Sopranos, Mezzos, Tenors, Bassos, and Other Friends

Sopranos, Mezzos, Tenors,

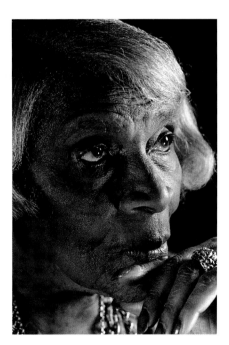

Bassos, and Other Friends

BY SCHUYLER CHAPIN

PHOTOGRAPHS AND CAPTIONS
BY JAMES-DANIEL RADICHES

CROWN PUBLISHERS NEW YORK

ALSO BY SCHUYLER CHAPIN

Musical Chairs: A Life in the Arts
Leonard Bernstein: Notes from a Friend

The author gratefully acknowledges permission to reprint the following:

"Anyone Can Whistle," by Stephen Sondheim. Copyright © 1964 (renewed) by Stephen Sondheim. Burthen Music Company, Inc., Owner of Publication and Allied Rights throughout the World, Chappell & Co., Sole Selling Agent. All Rights Reserved. Used by Permission.

The Last Prima Donnas, by Lanfranco Rasponi. Copyright © 1982 by Lanfranco Rasponi. Reprinted by permission of Alfred A. Knopf, Inc.

Sondheim & Company, by Craig Zadan. Copyright © 1989 by Craig Zadan. Reprinted by permisssion of HarperCollins Publishers.

Published by Crown Publishers, Inc., 201 East 50th Street, New York, New York 10022. Member of the Crown Publishing Group

Random House, Inc. New York, Toronto, London, Sydney, Auckland

CROWN is a trademark of Crown Publishers, Inc.

Printed in Singapore

Design by June Bennett-Tantillo

Library of Congress Cataloging-in-Publication Data
Chapin, Schuyler.
Sopranos, mezzos, tenors, bassos, and other friends / by Schuyler Chapin; photographs by James-Daniel Radiches.—1st ed.
1. Singers—Biography. 2. Singers—Portraits. I. Radiches, James-Daniel. II. Title.
ML400.C466   1995
782.1'092'2—dc20
[B]   94-32068
CIP
ISBN 0-517-58864-1

10   9   8   7   6   5   4   3   2   1

First Edition

Contents

The Tenors and Bassos

And Other Friends

Prologue

*In which I offer the background of this book,
introduce James Radiches, tell a story about Callas,
and dedicate the texts, with affection, to my friends
Pat and Bill and Peter*

The genesis of this opus goes back to a sweltering September evening in 1984, when my wife and I were lolling on a seventy-foot sailing yacht moving slowly over the oily swells of the Hudson River. We were supposed to be under canvas; with no wind we were moving at a leisurely pace on engine power.

Our group was a lively one, assembled by Pat and Bill Buckley—he founder of *National Review,* columnist, lecturer, novelist, and a recognized authority on ocean sailing, and she one of New York's most elegant hostesses. With their unerring instinct for picking company, our fellow passengers included editors, a thoughtful television commentator, several authors, two university deans, a diplomat, an international banker, a performing musician, and a soprano. The food was delicious, the wine perfect—a summer night's delight.

During part of the voyage, the soprano pressed me on some matter to do with the Metropolitan Opera where, from 1972 until 1975, I was general manager, and actually the last person to hold that post with its traditional authority over both artistic and administrative matters. As I recall, she was put out, in that way singers are often put out, about something I had or had not done; probably my failure to engage her services. In any event, to prevent one of those confrontational operatic melodramas, I led her away from her grievances by telling a few stories about things that actually happened during my time at that august theater, including a wild adventure involving Maria Callas.

This particular adventure began in the winter of 1974, when George Moore, then president of the Met's board of directors, gave birth to the idea that Callas should become the company's artistic director. He called me from his home in Sotogrande, Spain, and in his usual unsubtle way ordered me to launch this project.

A few days after Moore's call, Callas arrived in New York. I invited her to lunch, taking care to send a car to fetch her, and we met at the Oak Room in the Plaza Hotel. Dressed in a matching strawberry-colored skirt and jacket, her black hair pulled into a neat bun, she wore a large ruby ring on the ring finger of her right hand, simple but elegant gold earrings, and businesslike discreet makeup. She was playing the executive and had the trappings just right.

She started our conversation by telling me that everything about the Metropolitan was wrong; the casting, conductors, stage directors, designers, chorus, dancers, public relations—all this had to be changed. She went on talking as she squinted at the menu, held close to her face because, as I soon discovered, she was maddeningly farsighted. Finally she rummaged in her purse for glasses, which at once gave her face an extraordinarily schoolmarmish look. She soon polished off a good lunch and agreed that she would come to that night's performance of *Otello,* with James Levine conducting James McCracken, Pilar Lorengar, and Sherrill Milnes in the beautiful Franco Zeffirelli production.

She arrived at the opera house just as the first act was ending, making a whispered-apology entrance into my box. She was, of course, instantly recognized by the people sitting in the two adjoining boxes, causing quite a stir. She listened to Otello's impassioned *"E tu m'a m'avi mie sventure . . ."*—a melody quickly taken up by Desdemona as it develops into one of Verdi's great love duets. McCracken and Lorengar were in splendid voice, and Levine's support from the pit was sensuous.

When the curtain fell, we adjourned to my office. Once seated, champagne glass in hand, she made it clear she thought the production appalling, McCracken impossible, Lorengar hopeless, and Levine inadequate but at least promising. She then announced she wasn't staying for the second act because of a birthday party, but we should plan to meet the next day to start our work. Then she swept out. I looked at my wife, shrugged my shoulders, and began organizing for that next day.

I'd realized from Moore's first call that this was an unworkable idea, but now having met the lady I knew the matter had to be handled very carefully. I therefore asked each of the department heads to come to my office the next afternoon at fifteen-minute intervals, starting with the artistic administration and working through the entire company, including business affairs, subscription, touring, legal, rehearsal planning, costumes, scenery, stagehands, public relations, box office, and front-of-the-house personnel (ushers, guides, etc.).

When she arrived I explained that we were a repertory house, playing five different operas seven times a week; that we had an orchestra of over 110 with "steady extras" on call as needed, a large chorus, a sizable company of dancers, and a considerable roster of *comprimàrios* (artists under contract who sing the supporting roles); and that the coordination of this effort was what made it possible to bring the curtain up every weeknight and twice on Saturdays. She looked startled; by the time she'd seen five department heads, her eyes glazed over. I then told her the financial facts of life and that we should begin right away to redo the next three seasons if we were going to carry out the changes she would undoubtedly want to make. At this point she smiled wanly and, rising from her chair, said she was flying back to Spain that evening and would report everything to George Moore.

I walked her to her car (which I'd provided every day of her visit) and kissed her on both cheeks. The car drove off, and I never heard another word on this subject.

I finished off the story by reminding everyone that with all her quirks, demons, and phobias, when Maria Callas was on the stage she dominated her audience, commanding it with the power of her overwhelming personality. She was always a star, the Judy Garland of serious music, whom the general and artistic public watched with fascination.

I must have been fairly seductive telling this tale because our fellow passengers seemed fascinated. At the end there was laughter, some poignancy, and increased curiosity.

Later that night, returning to port, Pat Buckley motioned to me to sit by her. She came to the point: the stories I'd been telling should not be lost or forgotten; I must put them into a book. No sooner had she finished than up came fellow guest Peter Duchin saying essentially the same thing. When we reached our berth, our host, standing at the gangway to bid his guests good night, told me that if I had any sense at all I would begin writing the book the very next day.

The next day indeed! Back in 1978 I'd written my autobiography, *Musical Chairs*, and spent almost a third of the book describing the Metropolitan Opera. Did I really have anything more to say about that institution? I thought about the matter for several months, and finally acknowledged that in the first book I had written a great deal about the politics of the Met but little about the nature of its artistic problems. How, in fact, *do* you cope with countless star singers, their egos, and their managers, the *comprimàrios,* the chorus, the dancers, the conductors, stage directors, choreographers, designers, and musicians, plus the myriad talented staff members who keep the seats filled, the subscribers happy, and the treasurer from having a stroke?

Looking back at the memoirs of other Metropolitan general managers—Giulio Gatti-Casazza and Sir Rudolf Bing, in addition to the biography of Edward Johnson—I saw that no one else had discoursed in any detail on those particular aspects of the job. And then there were many other artists not necessarily involved with the Metropolitan about whom I wanted to write, artists I'd known and worked with during a career in music management stretching back almost forty-five years.

While mulling all this over, I was visited one day by James Radiches, a highly charged young photographer who burst into my office with a collection of stunning photo portraits he'd taken of various operatic, theatrical, and musical artists. He sat down, telling me briskly he was there at the insistence of Dorothy Kirsten, who apparently felt that I was an ideal candidate to write the texts to go with his photographs. I told him I didn't write treacly apographs or pompous coffee-table essays.

But Radiches is not the type of man to be dissuaded. Finally, at the end of a particularly frustrating discussion, I picked up his photographs of Franco Corelli and told him to come back in two days and I'd have some kind of text for him. He smiled the smile of victory.

That night I went home and wrote about that grand, tempestuous tenor, trying in words to match the mood and style of the Radiches photographs. When I'd completed my task, I told the young man I was only interested in collaborating if we could agree on three points: first, the artists in the book would only be those with whom I'd actually worked, either at the Metropolitan or elsewhere, or they were to be artists with whom I had at least had some kind of collaborative relationship; second, the texts would basically reflect my personal experiences with the artists as opposed to lengthy and boring biographical essays; and third, if he had not photographed those artists I wanted to include who are no longer living, he would have to create photographic collages evoking the image and spirit of the particular person. He agreed, and without telling me rushed off to Crown to show the resourceful Betty Prashker our collaborative ideas. She at once supported our purposes.

All of this book, then, is about people, those glorious talents that have enriched our lives and brought beauty, joy, and order in a troubled, nervous, inattentive world. I pray that I have recorded here my gratitude to them.

Much has happened since I began this project. Betty Chapin, my wife of forty-seven years, died suddenly in 1993, but not before her keen eyes had seen and approved our efforts, including my desire to dedicate my part of this book to my three persistent friends whose initiative actually germinated the idea. I salute Betty's memory, and celebrate the ongoing lives of our four sons, Henry, Theodore, Sam, and Miles, and our nine grandchildren. They are the reasons for my continuing optimism about the crazed world we live in, a world where, finally, the arts will be the fingerprint of our civilization.

—Schuyler Chapin

Long Pond and New York City, 1994

The Sopranos and Mezzos

Birgit Nilsson

W hen the pages of post–World War II opera history are read by scholars and music lovers in the next century, I have a feeling the so-called golden age, starting in the early 1800s and continuing until just before World War I, may begin, finally, to be eclipsed. Not that I'm suggesting we've been living in an operatic superage, but rather that we have witnessed in our lifetime a rich cornucopia of talent who've left indelible marks on the history of this grand, glorious, slightly insane art form.

If one starts way back with Angelica Catalani, Giuditta Pasta, Maria Malibran, and Giulia Grisi, and moves through the nineteenth and early twentieth century with Jenny Lind, Adelina Patti, Nelly Melba, Jean and Edouard de Reszke, Enrico Caruso, Feodor Chaliapin, and the almost unmatched Wagnerians Kirsten Flagstad and Lauritz Melchior, we must now mix and match the artists of our own time. In my view these include, among others, Joan Sutherland, Renata Tebaldi, Franco Corelli, Marilyn Horne, Jon Vickers, Richard Tucker, Luciano Pavarotti, Placido Domingo, and without a moment's hesitation one of the most exciting voices of this or any other generation—Birgit Nilsson.

I first met Birgit Nilsson in 1964, when I was Lincoln Center's program officer. I was organizing a series of recitals in what is now Avery Fisher Hall, in an attempt to conquer by musical propaganda its original foul acoustic reputation. At the suggestion of Kurt Weinhold, her concert manager, I engaged Miss Nilsson to lead off the series.

Now, I must confess I made this booking with something other than pure artistic intent. I figured if her huge voice could be heard clearly all over the auditorium, the public might be persuaded the acoustics were not bad after all, despite *New York Times* critic Harold Schonberg's incessant attacks.

Needless to say, we were not disappointed. When she walked onto the stage and began singing, her voice reached every corner clearly and distinctly. After her performance she was exceedingly gracious about the hall as a splendid place to perform, but her opinions were not necessarily echoed by other artists or by the principal tenant, the New York Philharmonic. Shortly after her concert, the building was closed for what turned out to be a considerable series of major renovations.

After the first renovation, I worked with her again, this time involving the New York Philharmonic in one of its first springtime Promenade Concerts, a series conceived by the conductor André Kostelanetz. Kostelanetz engaged her to sing an all Richard Strauss concert, ending with the final scene from *Salome*. When that began, either maestro Kostelanetz had trouble hearing his players or just suddenly decided to let all orchestral forces fly; whatever it was, in a matter of seconds Miss Nilsson could not be heard over the din of the musicians. She sensed something wrong and, while singing, turned to look at the maestro, a puzzled expression on her face. He remained oblivious, caught up in the throes of Strauss's orchestral hurricane. She even stepped back a pace or two, trying to catch his attention, but without success. Suddenly she'd had enough and, moving forward to center stage, tossed back her head and let fly with her own increase in volume, her voice sailing out over the orchestra. Kostelanetz turned abruptly to look at her. With unmistakable fire in her eyes, she made it clear she was prepared to sing at her present volume all night, if that was needed. The maestro received the message; suddenly the orchestra retreated, and with its return to normal Straussian chaos, Nilsson, too, reduced her volume. The dynamics were brought under control, or at least as much control as that wild score will allow, and the scene was brought to a splendid conclusion. Backstage I murmured something to her about the hall's continuing acoustical difficulties. She just winked.

"Conductors have acoustical problems," she said. "Singers don't!"

After that stirring rendezvous it was some eight years before our paths crossed again, and when they did I was the acting general manager of the Metropolitan Opera, her spiritual and professional home in America. On her arrival for the 1972–1973 season, where she was to sing in *Die Walküre* and *Siegfried,* she immediately came to my office to reassure me that commitments made to her old friend Goeran Gentele, my immediate predecessor, were also commitments made to me. Since our plans called for another Ring cycle in 1974–1975, to say nothing of a major revival of *Tristan und Isolde* for 1973–1974, this was good news indeed.

During that visit, over a cup of tea, I had a chance to put a delicate question to her prompted by professional need and personal interest.

"How long," I asked, "do you intend to continue your career?"

I went on to explain I had once asked Jascha Heifetz that question, in the days when I was his tour manager. Heifetz replied he would continue playing as long as he felt he was meeting his own standards.

"That will do for me," she replied. And then, characteristically, she smiled. "As long as the birds are happy, they will sing!"

When I think back on those days I'm reminded again how the word *professional* is correctly used when one thinks of Birgit Nilsson. She was never careless about her responsibilities, always working hard and giving full attention to the smallest detail. She also seemed to manage well the difficult balancing act between being an artist and an individual human being. Her unquenchable sense of humor often emerged in tight situations; here are a couple of examples.

Early in the Met's 1968–1969 season, prior to the infamous strike, Herbert von Karajan was beginning to light, stage, and conduct a new Ring; Nilsson was scheduled to sing all the Brunnhildes. During rehearsals for *Die Walküre,* she objected to what seemed like more light on the conductor than on the stage. Just before the premiere performance, a friend presented her with a miner's helmet, complete with battery-operated headlight. After the final curtain she donned the helmet, turned on the headlight, and rushed to Karajan's dressing room.

BIRGIT NILSSON

New York City
April 16, 1986

"Anything but farming!" she said, laughing, her sense of humor in tow when I suggested we change pose. Remembering that Nilsson grew up on a farm in Sweden, I asked her about those—halcyon?—days, and she recounted an anecdote concerning her father, a farmer who liked to profess that *farming* took precedence over "singing": "One of the very first performances my father saw of me was with Jussi Björling in *Tosca*. And when the public applauded me there, he turned around and said: 'Oh, you shouldn't applaud *her*—that's only my daughter'!" We finished photographing. Nilsson brought out a basket containing different types of beer. Together we shared a Munich lager.   —J.D.R.

"With this on my head, I'll be able to find my way onstage during the next performance!" was her remark to him.

He was not amused.

After the premiere, Karajan insisted his dressing room be relocated from the traditional conductor's suite to rooms near the principal artists'; he was annoyed by the sound of musicians tuning before a performance. Since *Die Walküre*'s Brunnhilde doesn't appear until the second act, Nilsson usually arrived at the theater a few minutes before the opera started. At the second performance she arrived in a happy mood, singing and yodeling down the corridor to her own dressing room. There she was greeted by the wardrobe mistress who told her, in hushed whispers, that the maestro was next door and she would have to be quiet as he didn't want to be disturbed by any sound.

"What is he going to do if I sneeze?" she whispered.

Once, years later, Karajan told me that Nilsson was only interested in money.

"You open her mouth and pour in money and then everything is fine," he said.

Once, also, when he was in desperate need of her talents, he sent a cable that went on for three full, single-spaced pages about how they should celebrate art and make music together, giving operas and dates before a final, flowery closing message. She sent back a two-word reply: "Busy. Birgit."

Watching her work, and getting to know her, became one of the pleasures of my first Met season. It wasn't long before I discovered that underneath her strength and professional expertise was a thinking and caring woman.

All this came into focus the day she visited my office to discuss the details of our future plans. I rather expected her to arrive with a battery of aides and was surprised when she walked in alone, carrying what can only be described as an old-fashioned Gladstone bag. She was wearing an elegant but subdued fur coat and over her head—this being wintertime and a slushy, rainy day as well—a bright scarf covered by a plastic rain hat. She apologized for dripping water on my carpet and as she sat down I noticed, really for the first time, that she was extremely attractive. I guess I must have stared a bit because in a moment she looked at me and laughed.

We began our discussions feeling relaxed. When our talk turned to precise dates, she opened the Gladstone and pulled out a handful of black-covered notebooks, laying them on the table in front of her with administrative precision.

"I have everything I need right here," she commented. "In opera I keep my own schedules and make my own bookings. My managers worry about concerts. This way I take direct responsibility for my opera commitments all over the world."

"But what if your managers book concerts that clash with your opera dates?" I asked, thinking back to my days as a concert agent.

"That doesn't happen," she replied, "I give the managers certain time periods for orchestra concerts and recitals and they book them. I decide when I shall sing opera and they leave those weeks to me. I tell them when I'll take holidays. These days are sacred! Now, let's talk about the next seasons."

And we did, sorting out rehearsals and performance dates, conductors and casts, and generally attending to her Metropolitan business with dispatch. At several times in our conversation I asked various members of the artistic administration to join us, and in what seemed like no time at all details for the three seasons ahead were in good order.

As she readied herself to leave, she made what seemed almost a casual comment about *Tristan und Isolde.* This particular production, described by one critic as "achingly beautiful," had been one of the glories of Sir Rudolf Bing's final year and was, as already noted, scheduled for a revival in the 1973–1974 season. The first three performances were to be sung by Catarina Ligendza with Jess Thomas and Jon Vickers alternating as Tristan. Nilsson and Vickers were to be together for the fourth and fifth presentations; arrangements for this had been completed before Gentele's death.

"Do you know Ligendza?" she asked.

"No, I don't," I replied, "I've heard her a number of times, but never worked with her."

"Be careful," she murmured, as I helped her on with her coat. "She's very nervous. I think she's afraid of New York."

I thanked her for her comment, little realizing how ghastly accurate she was going to be.

Nilsson's first performance under my management was in *Siegfried* on November 17, 1972. The production itself was to have premiered in 1969, but Karajan refused to return to the Met after the strike. He did suggest to Bing, and later to Gentele and myself, that we engage his assistant, Wolfgang Weber, to take over his directorial chores; we agreed because Weber, an extremely talented young man, was familiar with both the maestro's ideas and our production's physical sets, which had been completed before the strike took place. Gentele offered the conducting assignment to Erich Leinsdorf, and on that November night he entered the pit to be greeted warmly by the orchestra and public alike.

Siegfried, the third opera of Wagner's Ring, is often regarded as the most difficult to sustain, both musically and dramatically. Brunnhilde doesn't enter until the third act, and when she does she's seen asleep on a mountaintop, surrounded by the fire Wotan summons at the close of *Die Walküre.* Siegfried climbs the mountain and discovers her while singing perhaps the greatest understatement in all of Wagner—*"Das ist kein Mann!"* He kisses her; she awakens to greet the sun and light and hail Siegfried, her savior.

That November night will always remain one of starkest terror to me, intermixed with relief and pleasure in reconfirming Nilsson's human qualities.

The performance went smoothly, up until the moment in the third act when Jess Thomas as Siegfried, having thrust the Wanderer aside, began his ascent to the summit. Just as he'd sung *"Jetzt loch ich ein liebes Gesell!"* the little telephone, placed in my box for emergencies, began ringing. I answered it quickly. The stage manager, in tense tones, told me we had a big problem. The stage ring, on which Siegfried was walking, was stuck in the open position; the machinery had fouled and there was no way we could notify Jess that he was, literally, about to fall into an abyss.

I dashed quickly backstage and stood by as the crew chief and four of his men crept under the set in an attempt to close the gap by hand. I looked onstage to see Jess walking majestically up the ramp, eyes fixed on the summit, the overpowering music making it impossible to catch his attention. I looked up toward the summit and saw Nilsson, her eyes turned downward, obviously staring at the unclosed opening. I looked at the stagehands frantically pushing the steel frame, two on each side of the hole, but it was only coming together at a snail's pace. Step by step, Jess was getting closer to Armageddon. I told the stage manager we were not about to have an accident, even if he and I had to stand up, in full view of the audience, and grab Jess's ankles. We were getting ready to do just that when, with final shoves, the two sections jolted close enough to allow Jess's left foot to touch the forward edge of the hole and his right to cross over safely. Another quick look upward revealed that Nilsson had closed her eyes; I imagined her sigh of relief.

When Siegfried reached the summit and determined that Brunnhilde was, indeed, a woman, she arose slowly and with solemn gestures saluted the earth and sky as she began singing that great paean to nature, *"Heil dir, Sonne! Heil dir, Licht!"* I noticed she seemed to tremble a little, most unusual for an artist of her professional certainty. I could see the sleeves of her tunic in what could only be described as a nervous flutter. Slowly she regained confidence, and as the scene drew to a close both of them were singing to each other with all the passion called for by the score. The curtain came down to enormous applause.

As the principals gathered for their curtain calls I noticed Birgit's costume was damp, actually quite wet in some spots. She came over to me shaking her head.

"While I was lying on that mountain," she said softly, "I suddenly realized I hadn't performed the *Siegfried* Brunnhilde in almost four years, and then I saw the black hole where the set should have closed."

She looked down at her costume.

"And then I had a little . . ."

At this point a stagehand brought her the usual small cold beer she always drank right after singing and before her bows. She immediately tilted the bottle, letting the contents dribble over her tunic. Quickly she exclaimed: "Oh, look at me! I've spilt beer all over the place."

She twisted and bunched together much of the offending cloth, and then shaking her head and indicating her clumsiness to the backstage group, went out in front of the curtain to be greeted by cheers and bravos.

Not another word was spoken, but when she'd taken her last bow she took my arm and we walked to her dressing room, where she entered and promptly closed the door. I waited outside a few minutes until she was ready to receive her guests, which she did clad in her dressing gown, looking as cool and collected as ever.

Nilsson's second appearance that season was in *Die Walküre* with a cast that included Gwyneth Jones as Sieglinde and Jon Vickers as Siegmund. Leinsdorf was again conducting, and unlike *Siegfried,* this performance proceeded with steady excitement. At its conclusion I was surprised when, in a somewhat hesitant way, Birgit asked to see me.

What was on her mind was simple and startling: during the 1974–1975

Ring cycle, instead of just performing Brunnhildes, she wanted to sing an occasional Sieglinde when Vickers was singing Siegmund. What did I think about this?

I told her I thought the idea magnificent: New York would then have a rare chance to hear the best heldentenor and dramatic soprano of our time as Wagner's tenderest lovers in next season's *Tristan und Isolde* and, a season later, in *Die Walküre.* We shook hands on the spot, both agreeing, for the time being, to keep this plan to ourselves.

Her remaining performances in *Siegfried* and *Die Walküre* proceeded without further adventures. After her last appearance, we had a delightful dinner together and a final meeting to confirm the specific changes in the 1974–1975 Ring. I also took the moment to tell her how much I was looking forward to next season's *Tristan,* confessing it was my favorite opera and that I could hardly wait to hear her together with Vickers. I little knew then what unbelievable adventures we would go through before that magic moment occurred.

As it turned out the Metropolitan's *"Tristan* crisis" (as the press dubbed it) began smoothly enough. Catarina Ligendza and Jon Vickers were scheduled for the first performances beginning in January 1974; Leinsdorf was to be the conductor. Since the production itself is highly complex and technically difficult—even dangerous—we invited the original designer, Gunther Schneider-Siemssen, and the director, August Everding, to oversee the revival. The first three performances were at a time when Nilsson was not available, hence the hiring of Miss Ligendza, who was to sing alternately with Vickers and Jess Thomas. All seemed in order, at least on paper, but as an extra precaution, and at the proper insistence of Leinsdorf, we engaged Doris Jung as both Ligendza's and Nilsson's understudy, or "cover," as understudies are referred to at the Metropolitan. It seemed a fairly foolproof plan. I should have known better.

At 12:30 P.M. on December 24, 1973, the first explosion occurred. Just as I was preparing to leave for Christmas in the country, my secretary, Peggy Tueller, entered my office with a telex message she'd just torn from the machine. Her face was pale, and without a word she handed me the paper.

"Regret my doctor forbids travel to the United States at this time due to intestinal infection. I must therefore cancel Isoldes for this season. Merry Christmas and Happy New Year. Catarina Ligendza."

"But what is this?" I finally exclaimed. "I just talked to her last week to reconfirm everything, and she sounded fine."

"She did this to Bing, too," Peggy remarked, "and in just the same manner. I think she's afraid of New York."

"That's just what Nilsson warned me about," I replied.

We were now faced with a real problem. Rehearsals were scheduled to begin the day after Christmas, and Leinsdorf was already en route to New York from his home in Switzerland. In addition, we could not postpone the production because it was too complicated technically; the designer and director were also en route from Europe; and, above all, I wanted to protect the project for what I knew was going to be one of the supreme operatic moments of the decade, the New York appearance of Nilsson and Vickers in the title roles. I took off my overcoat and, returning to my desk, telephoned Betty that a real crisis had emerged and I had no idea when I would be free to leave. I then called the artistic administrative staff and broke the news to them.

Now these good people, all veterans of the Met's operatic wars, were thoroughly accustomed to dealing with such crises, but it's one thing to find a soprano who could pinch-hit as Mimi and quite another to find a substitute Isolde.

I began by calling Nilsson in Vienna, where she was appearing at the Vienna State Opera, and alerting her to our problem. She was warmly sympathetic but bound by contract to Vienna and there was no way of her coming to us until her scheduled time. She did suggest I try throwing myself on the mercy of Rudolf Gamsjager, the intendant of Vienna, whom I knew quite well, and I, indeed, did so. Gamsjager chuckled at my distress, clucked understandingly about my problem, and absolutely refused to release Nilsson from her obligations to him.

My colleagues, meanwhile, were burning up the wires to Europe, trying to reach every possible artist who had the part in their repertoire.

In the midst of all this I received a phone call from my friend Carlos Moseley, managing director of the New York Philharmonic. Could I help him out of a terrible jam? His Christmas week conductor had canceled and there was no one available except Leinsdorf. Could I lend him to the New York Philharmonic? I told Carlos of my problem and that Leinsdorf was due in New York at any moment. I was certain we could work out some arrangement.

Leinsdorf arrived that evening and was shocked by the news, asking why he had not been informed. I told him the telex arrived while he was already in the air. The look he gave me indicated the least I should have done was to arrange for his plane to make a midair return to Switzerland. I asked if he was aware of the New York Philharmonic problem and he told me Carlos had reached him and he'd agreed to take over the concerts. He presumed I wouldn't mind if he did this, pointing out he could prepare for and conduct the concerts without altering his Metropolitan rehearsal schedule. I told him I had no objection, secretly relieved he'd be busy and not a frequent visitor to the administrative offices while our Isolde search continued. I suggested he should begin his Met rehearsals with Doris Jung, whom he had insisted we hire, but he made it abundantly clear that Miss Jung was for emergencies, not premiere performances, and someone of major stature had better be identified immediately.

Christmas Day was not a happy one for any of us. I'd gone off to the country to be with my family as scheduled, figuring I could make as many telephone calls from my study as from my office. I did just that, leaving them to celebrate as best they could.

Obviously everyone in my immediate family had been caught willy-nilly in my problem. At one point someone jokingly reminded me our local fish market proprietor had a daughter who could sing. The day after Christmas, Betty and I visited his shop to pick up some lobsters. I asked him if his daughter sang Isolde. He looked somewhat blank but said he would ask her. I told him not to bother.

Meanwhile, back in New York, rehearsals were under way. Leinsdorf was forced to use Miss Jung because August Everding, the director, needed her for staging rehearsals with Vickers. Vickers, in turn, became extremely irritable when a Ligendza replacement was not instantly on hand and came to my office to inform me he wished to be relieved of his assignment until the crisis was solved. I told him that was impossible; he did not know the physical production, which in the second act is particularly dangerous as Tristan and Isolde are both strapped into bos'n chairs and lifted aloft. I suggested he should continue rehearsing as I was certain we would soon solve our problem. He didn't leave my office looking very happy, but right after he departed Peggy Tueller came in flourishing another cable. Usually that meant more bad news, but this time it turned out to be our first ray of hope. The cable was from the American soprano Klara Barlow, who was making quite a name for herself in various German opera houses. She had picked up the news of our difficulties and now offered her services, effective immediately. She knew the Ligendza performance dates and had cleared her schedule to accept a Metropolitan invitation, should one be forthcoming.

I confess I'd never heard of Miss Barlow, but the members of the artistic administration knew all about her, and told me she had, in fact, replaced Ligendza in Met performances of *Fidelio* a few seasons back. I contacted Leinsdorf with this news, but he was, to put it mildly, less than enthusiastic, implying she was an adequate provincial soprano but not of Metropolitan stature. I then called Nilsson, who encouraged me by saying she had a fine reputation in Europe and should work well with both Vickers and Jess Thomas. That was all I needed to hear; I telephoned Miss Barlow and told her to come to New York immediately.

As soon as Leinsdorf heard about my decision, he bounded into my office with the news he had no intention of conducting for Klara Barlow unless she agreed to audition for him. He wished her to sing the entire first act of the opera. He graciously allowed that it would not be necessary to summon the orchestra and suggested Richard Woitach of the musical staff would be an acceptable alternative at the piano. He then took the occasion to remind me again how extremely disappointed he was with everyone and everything connected with the new Met management. I was, once again, glad he was busy, running back and forth between rehearsals at the Metropolitan and rehearsals and performances at the New York Philharmonic.

Miss Barlow arrived and I told her of Leinsdorf's demand. She shrugged and agreed, and we made the necessary arrangements. At the appointed hour a piano was moved onto the stage while Miss Barlow waited in the wings for the maestro's arrival. I asked the artistic administration to be present, as well as Everding and Schneider-Siemmsen. We all settled into the auditorium just as Leinsdorf appeared.

Without a word of welcome he nodded to Woitach and the audition began. When

KLARA BARLOW

*New York City
August 27, 1992*

I wanted to capture the essence of Isolde in Barlow's beauty . . . and I shot the photograph as the surging—and potent—music of Wagner's love duet swelled through the stereo.   —J.D.R.

it was completed—and she did sing the entire act—the maestro thanked Woitach, complimenting him on the beautiful completion of a Herculean task, and without one word to Miss Barlow marched out of the auditorium. I was appalled, and immediately went onstage to assure her she had been magnificent and welcome her back to the Metropolitan Opera. I then telephoned Nilsson, who was surprised and annoyed to hear my report but pleased Miss Barlow had succeeded.

The next day Leinsdorf and his wife, Vera, appeared in my office. They got down to business immediately: could he, please, be relieved from his contract? The whole Ligenzda problem was too much; he had been looking forward to happy experiences with the new management but everything had turned sour. Vera Leinsdorf, with constrained voice and tears, told of their anticipation of a high artistic experience and how Klara Barlow was going to dash those hopes. I reminded them that Miss Barlow was present to sing Ligenzda's performances only and, further, had agreed to stay on as a fully prepared extra cover for Nilsson, a bonus I thought extremely attractive. I also reminded them when Nilsson arrived we were to have the rare privilege of Nilsson and Vickers onstage together in this most special of all Wagner operas, and therefore I was sorry not to be able to grant their request. With looks of what I can only describe as disgust, they both took their leave.

I put in another call to Nilsson. I told her what happened and that I would not be surprised if he walked out on his commitments.

"Don't worry," she said reassuringly. "You have a young conductor in the house with whom I've performed the opera at least six times and I would be delighted to work with him again. He's a fellow countryman of mine."

"You mean Lief Segerstam?" I asked, mentioning a young man who was making his debut with us that season.

"Absolutely right," she responded. "He's first class. And don't worry about Jon. I'll take care of him. Just let me know what happens."

No sooner had I put down the phone than Vickers came in.

"Look here, Schuyler," he said, "this is all too much. I'm going back home to Bermuda. The maestro and I are very unhappy, and I'll return when Birgit gets here."

And with that he walked out.

He'd not been gone five minutes when the phone rang. It was the critic from the *New York Post* wanting to know just what was going on. She told me Vickers and Leinsdorf had just given a statement to the press announcing their resignations from the production and, among other observations, Leinsdorf was accusing me of being a "commissar of optimism." I said we were indeed having a few problems, but I was confident that calm and reason would return. When I put the phone down I realized, if I hadn't known it before, that I was in the middle of a real operatic war.

My next move was to contact Jess Thomas, who was already scheduled to alternate with Vickers during the run. I explained what was happening and asked if he'd take over the premiere.

"Of course I will," came the generous reply. "Klara's a good colleague. Don't worry about a thing. We'll be just fine." I thanked him for his understanding and for his good spirit.

Then came a call from Sheldon Gold, Leinsdorf's manager and an old friend. He began by telling me he was going to ask something that was none of his business but was obviously very important.

"If Leinsdorf doesn't show up tomorrow," he said, "do you have someone to take his place?"

"You're right," I replied. "It is none of your business, but the answer is yes."

There was a long pause before Gold said he would get back to me later that day.

While all this was going on, Schneider-Siemmsen and Everding were doing the best they could under battle circumstances to mount the production on the stage. They worked with Klara Barlow and, until he left in a huff, Vickers. With Vickers's departure, Jess Thomas came in immediately. I wasn't particularly worried about him as he had sung most of the performances with Nilsson during the last Bing season, but I was worried about Vickers, who was still not familiar enough with this tricky production. I found he had not yet actually skipped off to Bermuda and telephoned his hotel.

He was courteous, even a little sheepish when he came on the phone. I told him what was on my mind.

"For your own safety," I said, "you should come in for technical rehearsals to learn the production. When Nilsson arrives there will only be time for touch-ups. You'll be at a terrible disadvantage if you're unfamiliar with the sets and props."

"All right," he said grudgingly, "but I won't sing."

"Suit yourself," I replied.

As promised, Sheldon Gold called back. Our conversation was brief.

"The maestro will be at his rehearsals tomorrow," he reported.

"Good," I said. "I'll be happy to greet him in the morning."

"I wouldn't do that, if I were you," he responded. "Stay far away from him. You'll be a lot happier if you do."

Good advice it was, too. Leinsdorf returned in a truculent mood affecting everyone concerned with the production. Vickers was persuaded to rehearse each act in costume and with orchestra, and while he didn't very often sing out, when he did I knew all the Sturm und Drang was going to be worthwhile.

In the late afternoon of the day Leinsdorf returned, Donal Henahan, then a music reporter at the *New York Times,* called for an interview. He was filled with gossip and innuendo, having talked with both the maestro and Vickers, and he let me know immediately the story was all over town that the Metropolitan was falling apart. While he didn't say as much, I sensed he'd also been talking with some of the trustees and was now looking for blood, probably mine. I took a deep breath, sighed, and told him to come to my office.

That interview was one of the strangest of my life. Henahan arrived, whipped out his pad and pencil, and suggested I begin at the beginning. I decided to do just that, and went through the *Tristan* saga step-by-step. I sat behind my desk and kept my voice casual, as if the whole story were no more than a routine day's work. With each question I was calm and in control.

By the time I'd finished, Henahan was intrigued.

"What are you going to do if Barlow gets sick and has to cancel?" he asked.

"Get out there and sing the role myself," was my reply. "I'll do just about anything to keep this production on the stage for the Nilsson-Vickers performances."

Henahan looked at me carefully.

"You really mean that, don't you!" he said.

"You're damn right I do," I answered.

He began to smile. "I brought a photographer with me," he added. "He's just outside. May I bring him in?"

"Be my guest," I answered.

Meanwhile down on the stage, Act III, in costume and with the orchestra, was in rehearsal. I had a little speaker on my desk hooked up to the stage sound system. I could hear the beginning of Tristan's great narrative and hurried down to the back of the house just in time to watch Leinsdorf bring the music to a halt and yell backstage at the stage manager, who was helping Schneider-Siemmsen adjust the lighting.

"What is this, amateur night?" he snarled. "I thought all this work had been done!"

Quietly the stage manager came out, explaining that a technical problem had developed but would be solved without interrupting either the stage action or the orchestra. Leinsdorf made no reply, but I could feel the tension spreading.

He resumed conducting, but a few moments later I saw a shadowy figure walk down the center aisle and go over to whisper something in his ear. He cocked his head to listen and Vickers spotted this conversation while lying on his bearskin bed. He immediately got to his feet and walked downstage.

"What is this, a union meeting?" he called out in a rage. "This is supposed to be my rehearsal!"

Leinsdorf looked up, pushed the man away, and apologized. The two men stared at each other for a moment, then Vickers went slowly back to his stage position and the rehearsal continued.

After about fifteen minutes I returned to my office to telephone Nilsson and bring her up-to-date. Suddenly she burst out laughing, and as she did I heard her say I was certainly getting a proper baptism in the world of the opera intendant.

"Hang on," she said. "You're doing just fine. I know everything will be all right. Keep your courage!"

The next day the Henahan article appeared, and it was extremely sympathetic to my position. With that I sensed a new feeling of support growing throughout the company. Over the next few days artists, technicians, staff, even a few board members stopped by to wish me well. Much to my surprise I began getting support mail from the public, including a generous and thoughtful letter from Carlos Moseley, who reminded me that despite all the problems, the music-loving public was generally sympathetic to the underdog. He encouraged me to stand firm and predicted that Barlow's premiere would be a triumph.

And a triumph it was, as reported on the front page of the *New York Times*. Barlow received a standing ovation at the end of each act, and those were the days when standing ovations were rarer than they are today. But despite her success in the face of considerable odds, Leinsdorf never once spoke to her. He would come onstage to take his bows and ignore her completely, a churlishness I've rarely seen in any professional situation. Barlow was, naturally, deeply hurt by his attitude but never said a word. She also never said a word about the fact that she gave her first performance with a temperature of 103°F.—a plucky lady, who sang four performances, including the broadcast, before Nilsson arrived.

Incidentally, the broadcast performance managed to smoke Vickers out of his

Bermuda home. Perhaps he felt he needed at least one performance under his belt before joining Nilsson or he didn't want to lose out on being heard by the national radio public or he realized he was sacrificing a lot of money by staying away; whatever the reason he suddenly appeared in New York and notified us he was ready to resume his schedule. At the end of the matinee he also made it clear that he was, in no way, going to appear the following Monday to rehearse with Nilsson. Charles Riecker, the artistic administrator, reminded him that Nilsson was arriving over the weekend especially for those rehearsals, but he only glared.

On the Sunday night of that weekend, my home phone rang about 6:30 P.M. with the cheery voice of Nilsson announcing she'd arrived safely and was looking forward to her rehearsals the following morning.

"There's only one thing," she said quietly. "I hear Jon may not show up. If this is so, I won't sing the performances with him."

I gulped.

"You understand," she went on, "this is a very difficult production and we must work out all our business together."

I told her I was certain he'd be there, even though my heart was rapidly sinking.

Monday morning at breakfast I sat quietly at our kitchen table drinking my tea, not saying anything but gloomy that despite all our efforts the Nilsson-Vickers *Tristan* was not to be. Betty sat opposite me drinking her coffee and suddenly, as if reading my mind, she said, "You're worried about the rehearsal. Don't be. I know he will turn up."

"How can you be so certain?" I murmured. "He's such a law unto himself."

"Please try not to worry," she repeated. "You'll see. He'll be at the theater."

I walked to work that Monday morning feeling defeated, but when I arrived at my office Riecker was there, grinning, with the news that Vickers was in the house, raising hell that his rehearsal schedule was wrong and he'd arrived an hour early.

"I took the paper and showed him he'd misread it," Riecker reported. "He's gone backstage to the coffee machines. Everything will be okay."

And it was. On the night of January 30, 1974, operatic history was made when

Birgit Nilsson and Jon Vickers finally appeared on the stage of the Metropolitan in *Tristan und Isolde.* Perhaps the best description of that night comes from Leinsdorf's own memoirs: "It is of no purpose to attempt a verbal account of an evening such as this one turned out to be. I am sure that in every diary this date will have a special place. Everything smiled on our endeavor, and I am glad to have been a part of it." A-men.

During her distinguished career at the Metropolitan, Birgit Nilsson sang every major Wagner role. During my time, however, one was missing: Brunnhilde in *Götterdammerung.* This event was scheduled after her *Tristan* triumphs, and she was looking forward to presenting her interpretation to the New York public. She was also pleased that Jess Thomas was to be her Siegfried and Rafael Kubelik the conductor.

Rehearsals began with high anticipation and proceeded smoothly until the morning of the first piano dress. This particular rehearsal, with the cast in costume and makeup and the orchestra replaced by a single piano, is to allow everyone to become familiar with the stage blocking—entrances, exits, and that sort of thing—together with the special movements required by the stage director. I usually did not attend; I knew I could always be called if needed and for that purpose I kept the intercom speaker at the side of my desk at low volume. I remember hearing the music heralding Brunnhilde's entrance and her opening and subsequent singing with Siegfried, and then I became aware that everything had stopped. I didn't think very much about it; interruptions are normal on such occasions. But this one seemed to go on a bit longer than most. I thought I heard what sounded like gasps from somewhere around the stage, but before I could reflect on this my office door was flung open by an obviously distraught Peggy Tueller. Pale and shaking, she spoke in almost hysterical tones, telling me there had been a ghastly accident on stage and I was needed immediately.

"It's Birgit," she said, as we were running toward the auditorium. "She's had a bad fall. We've already sent for an ambulance. She's in great pain."

"Where is she?" I asked, as we reached the stage.

"Over there," she said, pointing to a broken ladder. "We haven't moved her. She was on those steps that gave way. She's lying at the bottom of them."

I went quickly to her side and saw immediately that something was very wrong. Her right shoulder blade was sticking out at what looked like a ninety-degree angle. She was obviously in great pain, moaning quietly, tears running down her face and forming little gullies which creased her makeup. She looked up at me just as the ambulance attendants were approaching, and when they began moving her she let out a scream that could be heard throughout the building. Everyone on stage was transfixed, many having rushed out when the accident occurred, and the stagehands, likewise, stood in little groups looking horrified and helpless. I told Peggy, who was a great personal friend of Nilsson's, to ride in the ambulance and see that everything was all right when they reached the hospital.

After the stretcher had been carried out I directed that the rehearsal continue with Rita Hunter, Nilsson's cover. An opera house is a superstitious place; I knew there might be emotional difficulties unless things returned to normal as soon as possible.

Later that afternoon I went to the hospital and found Nilsson had just returned from the operating room, where her shoulder—which had been separated—had been put back in place using a complicated procedure that required a general anesthetic. When I entered the room she was in bed with a blanket and sheet pulled up under her chin. She looked strange—dark faced, with deep black canals running down the sides of her face and under her eyes. Tufts of hair were sticking out in all directions; her nose seemed sharp, almost pointed. She looked exhausted, an old woman. I approached her bed cautiously. As I drew near I realized the hospital, while removing her costume and most of her wig, had neglected to wash off her stage makeup. The effect was startling, as if the Mona Lisa had been created by Baron Frankenstein.

When I returned later in the evening she was sitting up, pale but composed.

"The nurse says you saw me with all the makeup," she said with a grin. "What a mess."

"Yes, but you look fine now," I replied.

"I feel sore all over and stiff and I'm very tired. We should talk in the morning." She waved a wan good-bye.

And in the morning, with the story of her accident on the front pages and blaring from the radio and television, and her room looking like the front window of a flower shop, we decided to wait before making any decisions about *Götterdammerung*. She did ask, very quietly and in a low voice, how I felt about the premiere. I said as far as I was concerned she would sing it if she felt up to doing it.

"We'll see," she answered, "we'll see."

Fortunately the premiere was ten days away and over those days we talked several times. It was obvious she wanted to sing, but only if she was physically up to it. We finally agreed to make the decision at 4:00 P.M. on the premiere afternoon.

"I know it's close," she said on the telephone, "and you better not have Miss Hunter in Philadelphia, but I think I'm going to be all right. We still have two days to go."

Twenty-four hours before the final decision, Rita Hunter, accompanied by her husband and daughter, appeared in the office with an ultimatum: either I decide immediately who sings the premiere or, and here she lowered her voice for dramatic effect, she might find it necessary to be indisposed as a cover.

"This is all a terrible strain," she murmured, "my nerves are frayed."

I listened to this musical blackmail, thinking how much I would like to strangle the lady, but then my tension eased as I looked at all three of them. Miss Hunter looked like the model for the late *New Yorker* cartoonist Otto Soglow's "Little King." So did her husband. And their daughter. I decided to take a chance.

"Miss Nilsson will be singing and you're expected to be in the theater in case of any problems, just as it says in your contract," I said, getting up from behind my desk and coming over to shake hands with each of them.

I must say she looked quite relieved, but I now knew my statement would be all over the house in a flash. I crossed my fingers.

Nilsson did indeed sing that premiere, with her right arm strapped to her side. When she made her entrance the audience burst into applause, something rarely, if ever, done at New York Wagner performances. As she started singing she sounded as if she were gargling; I suddenly had the panicked thought that she wasn't going to make it, but after a few moments her voice rang out clear and powerful as always.

Everything was incredible, including all the stage business, until the beginning of the immolation scene, when it was obvious as she began that she was out of energy and out of voice. I watched her struggle on technique alone, like a Rolls-Royce running down a highway on its wheel rims. When the curtain finally came down she almost fainted from exhaustion.

JESS THOMAS

Tiburon, California
October 27, 1991

Jess Thomas wrote: "Wagner's work [*Tristan und Isolde*] is soul-searching. And in the psyche, extremes always have their counterpoise. The great problem we face from birth is death, the giving up of what we've come to know as the self." Two years later almost to the day I had photographed him, Jess Thomas was dead.   —J.D.R.

The cold glass of beer, unspilled this time, revived her enough that she could take her curtain calls, and when they were finished I walked her slowly back to her dressing room. On the way I asked what happened at her entrance. She stopped in her tracks.

"You remember when the audience started to applaud?" she asked. "I began crying. I turned to Jess Thomas and whispered in his ear I couldn't go on. Do you know what he did? He squeezed my good arm and whispered in my ear, 'Oh, yes you can, baby.' What a colleague!"

It's hardly necessary to add that the next morning the critics were all over themselves with praise for her vocal splendor, her pluck, and her endurance.

That wasn't the only close call between Nilsson and Wagner during my years as general manager. The next was on February 20, 1975, at the first performance of *Die Walküre,* when Nilsson and Vickers sang Sieglinde and Siegmund together for the first time. The audience was enraptured, but that was nothing compared to the pleasure Vickers displayed when he discovered the casting surprise she and I agreed upon the year before.

Jon Vickers, apart from his extraordinary voice, is a physically powerful man, with

square shoulders, tree-trunk legs, and strong hands. He was obviously delighted to be with Nilsson, and they sang and acted together with the same passion they'd shown in *Tristan und Isolde.* At the end of Act I, Vickers approached the ash tree in Hunding's house to pull out the sword, pulling it splendidly but giving it such an exuberant twist that the blade broke loose from the hilt and spun, end over end, into the air, whistling past Nilsson's nose and landing in the protective net over the orchestra pit. There were gasps from the audience, and I left my box posthaste to be backstage for the curtain.

I arrived just as Vickers was singing his final three lines—*"Braut und Schwester, bist du dem Bruder. So blühe denn, Walsungenblut!"* Wife and sister you'll be to your brother. So let the Volsung blood flourish!

"But not my blood, please, Jon!" said Nilsson just after the curtain came down.

Vickers was horrified. I reached them both just as he was giving Nilsson a hug and apology. Nilsson looked at me and was shaking.

"Did you see what happened?" she cried out. "If I hadn't moved my head, my nose would have been broken!"

After a minute or two she collected herself and they both went forward for their bows. I told the prop man the next sword better be bolted together or I suspected Nilsson might give Wagner a wide berth at the Metropolitan.

Birgit Nilsson's last performance for my management was the 1975 broadcast of *Götterdammerung* with Sixten Ehrling, an old colleague and friend of hers, as conductor. Ehrling was just fine with Birgit, who often worked with him in Stockholm and enjoyed his precision and unflappability.

That unflappability almost came apart, however, at the *Götterdammerung* orchestra dress rehearsal of Act II. With perhaps six people in the house, for some inexplicable reason the performance on stage began to take off. Each singer, from Nilsson to Jess Thomas to John Macurdy to Bengt Rundgren to Nell Rankin to Marius Rintzler began singing and acting as if their lives depended on it. Ehrling and the orchestra got caught up in this spirit, and at the end of the act no one moved from their places. The curtain came down slowly, the orchestra all remained seated, and the singers just kept looking at one another.

Ehrling came up from the pit and began speaking to Birgit in Swedish.

"I don't know," she replied in English, and looking over at her fellow artists asked, "What happened?"

"I don't know either," said Jess Thomas.

"Nor do I," added John Macurdy. "Maybe we just remembered we are all artists dealing with Wagner's genius. But, my God, I'll never forget this morning." And then he paused. "It was you, Birgit. You started it and we all got caught up."

He leaned down and kissed her. The others broke into applause. So did the orchestra. So did the six people in the auditorium.

Birgit Nilsson—one of the great singers of our time, a responsible artist who never cheated the public, who cut through acres of thick operatic nonsense, who knew her talents and limitations (although those were precious few), and never brought anything but pleasure to the operagoing public for over thirty-five years. She was—is—her own golden age.

Renata Tebaldi

It's an interesting historical fact that Renata Tebaldi, one of the great spinto sopranos of our time, began and ended her Metropolitan Opera career with the same role. Rudolf Bing introduced her to the New York public in 1955 as an unforgettable Desdemona opposite Mario del Monaco; her last performance, again Desdemona, was under my management on January 8, 1973, this time with James McCracken as her Otello. In the seventeen years between her debut and farewell, Tebaldi had what can best be described as a passionate and tumultuous love affair with the New York operagoing public, a love affair that was totally reciprocated.

Tall and elegant, Tebaldi never cheated, never undertook a role unless she felt it appropriate for her voice and temperament, and was totally unafraid to face down managers and impresarios who tried to persuade her otherwise (more about this later!). What fascinates me is that as a deeply committed Italian and grand diva of La Scala, La Fenice, and other great opera houses of Italy—to say nothing of Vienna, London's Covent Garden, and the Paris Opera—she found her greatest professional pleasure

in the United States: in San Francisco, where she made her American debut in 1950; in Chicago; but especially in New York.

RENATA TEBALDI

Milan, Italy
January 28, 1992

Four days before her seventieth birthday, I photographed Tebaldi at her apartment in Milan. Storefront windows throughout the city showcased her recordings alongside placards of greetings, heralding her birthday. The occasion itself culminated with an homage at La Scala. I remember Tebaldi turning to me between exposures, a mischievous glint in her eye . . . she was in a jocular mood. Suddenly inspired, holding bunches of silk flowers, she sang to the camera: *"Son pochi fiori, povera viole, son l'alito d'aprile dal profumo gentile. . . "* (Just a few flowers, humble violets, they are the breath of April with their tender fragrance . . .) The voice was profoundly moving—it was still "the voice of an angel."   —J.D.R.

Shortly before Tebaldi was born in the Italian city of Pesaro—coincidentally also the hometown of Rossini—her parents separated. As a result little Renata went to live with her mother and maternal grandparents in Langhirano, a small town near Parma. In her early years there was a brief reconciliation between her parents, but it didn't last. For a long time she thought her father, a cellist by profession, was dead. As a sensitive child she suffered terribly from this family discord, becoming more and more attached to and dependent upon her mother, Giuseppina.

What many people don't know is that at the age of three she was stricken with polio. As a growing youngster, she fought the disease with self-imposed discipline and determination, thus giving birth to a pattern of behavior that has always governed her personal and professional life.

Tebaldi began her musical education as a teenager, studying the piano privately in Parma but quickly discovering that her pianistic gifts were modest. What she really had was a voice. Her piano teacher persuaded her to audition for the conservatory in Parma as a singer; she was accepted, pretending to be eighteen, the age of admittance, when she was really only sixteen.

She studied singing there for almost two years before a major turning point in her life: she went off to spend a Christmas holiday with her father's brother, her uncle

Valentino, at Pesaro. There, as operatic destiny would have it, Valentino owned a small café where the famous former diva Carmen Melis came to buy pastries. Melis was a teacher at the Pesaro Conservatory, then the most celebrated in Italy.

Valentino talked to Melis about his niece, and the diva finally consented to audition the young girl. Still a prima donna *assoluta* in her own way, Melis terrified Tebaldi, who at this time was basically a simple country girl. But although Melis criticized her manner of singing, she agreed that the voice had a lovely timbre. The next day, and for the remainder of her holiday, Tebaldi worked with Melis; when she returned to Parma, the improvement was so drastic that no one believed it was the same voice.

It was then that she determined to move to Pesaro permanently, where she lived with her father's family and took classes with Melis both at the conservatory and privately. When Italy was dragged into World War II frequent bombings forced the conservatory to close. Melis moved off to live near Como, and Tebaldi, with her mother, moved deep into the countryside where she continued to vocalize on her own.

"La Signora Melis and I kept in touch as best we could," she told Lanfranco Rasponi in 1982, "and in 1944 she let me know that she had arranged for me to make my debut as Elena in *Mefistofele* in Rovigo, under the very well known conductor Giuseppe del Campo. I went to meet Melis ten days before the performance to study the role—a short one, but very effective—and she was perfectly marvelous; she never left me, even in the wings of the theater, until the curtain went up. There I was, on the couch, terrified. But la Signora was pleased with the results."

The debut was an important success, but wartime Italy was hardly encouraging to young singers. Tebaldi sang a few performances here and there, but it wasn't until 1946, when she appeared as Desdemona in Trieste with Francesco Merli, that the news spread like wildfire: a wonderful new voice had appeared on the horizon.

Tebaldi spoke about this moment in her own words: "Immediately all the theaters opened their doors to me, and it was thrilling for me that all the sacrifices my mother had made for me—she always would have preferred to see me married and settled— had not been in vain. Desdemona, until the end of my career, remained my favorite heroine: innocent, good-natured, the victim of love and jealousy, which know no laws."

As mentioned earlier, Renata Tebaldi was always part of a magical love affair between herself and her public. From her entrance to her final moment in a performance, she embraced the audience with commanding presence and her open smile. Communication was immediate and undeniable. Critics vied to describe her sound in terms ranging from rich and warm to delicate, sumptuous, glowing, velvety, womanly—all virtues bound to capture an adoring public. But it was a combination of all these qualities that made Tebaldi unique, for whether she let fly with heroic splendor or scaled down to a shimmering pianissimo, she always honored the score with scrupulous care for dynamics. These trademarks extended from the lyrical Mimi in *La Bohème* to the dramatic La Gioconda and Minnie in *La Fanciulla del West.* Early in her career, she had ventured into some Wagner as well, yet what she will be remembered for are her quintessential Italian roles: Tosca, Manon Lescaut, Madama Butterfly, Violetta, the *Forza* Leonora, La Gioconda, Adriana Lecouvreur, and, of course, Desdemona.

Before joining the Metropolitan I was one of those unabashed Tebaldi fans; shortly after joining the company, however, I realized I was going to have to be the one to suggest that it might be a wise idea for her to consider a different repertoire.

The day after a particularly harrowing Desdemona, I telephoned her hotel to ask if I might come to see her. She replied that it would be better if she came to my office, and we agreed on a date.

At the appointed hour she arrived, dressed in an elegant, subdued suit covered by a full-length dark mink coat. It was a cold, bright sunny winter day, and I remember thinking how strikingly attractive she was as she came through the door and I walked over to greet her.

We settled into comfortable seats and I began by telling her what pleasure she'd given to so many people over the exciting years of her career. She looked at me, acknowledging my comments with a slight nod, obviously waiting to discuss future plans. I then asked if she'd ever given thought to appropriate mezzo-soprano roles that might be compatible alternatives to her present repertoire.

At the mention of "mezzo-soprano" her back stiffened and her face froze. She did not say a word, just looked at me with thorough contempt and without further ado arose out of her chair, wrapped her fur coat around her with firm authority, and left the room.

Shortly after this unfortunate rendezvous, we saw each other once more. We were sitting in adjoining boxes at Carnegie Hall during a memorial concert celebrating the life of the impresario Sol Hurok. I nodded politely to her; she looked away. No words were spoken. I was saddened by such a rupture but understood.

Five years later, however, Renata Tebaldi reappeared in my life, not in person, but through what I can only describe as a crazed fan.

In April 1977 I was rushed to Roosevelt Hospital in New York with severe intestinal bleeding. Tests showed that a long-standing ulcer had bled for a second time; the doctors recommended a partial gastrectomy. Before this operation could be performed, however, around-the-clock blood tests were required, and in the middle of my first night I awoke to find a sinister-looking technician sitting alongside the right side of my bed, his tray of sharp instruments balanced on his lap, staring at me with what can only be described as loathing. Truth to say I was only vaguely awake after a drug-induced sleep, and thought perhaps my imagination was playing tricks. I extended my arm, which he examined roughly, finally finding a vein that would serve his purposes. He wrapped my arm painfully with a rubber tourniquet and, picking up a syringe with an enormous needle, said:

"Why didn't you bring back Tebaldi?"

"What? What did you say?" I asked, looking down at the needle and up at his face.

"I said, why didn't you bring back Tebaldi? You were cruel, you know. Very cruel." His face was a map of anger.

I instantly thought I was in the middle of a bad novel; but this was no novel. The man with the needle was deadly serious.

"Why don't you finish what you're doing?" I suggested quietly, suppressing my panic. "Then we can talk about that splendid artist."

He looked at me with no expression on his face but his eyes flashed anger. Slowly he put the needle into my vein and slowly he withdrew blood—very, very slowly. I hate needles; by instinct he must have known this. It seemed hours before he was finished.

When he undid the tourniquet, I told him about Tebaldi's vocal difficulties and that I'd suggested to her that she look at some mezzo-soprano roles. He made no comment, just squirted my blood into test tubes. I went on about how much I admired her and how sorry I was that we never had a second conversation.

By this time he'd finished his tasks, still with no further remarks to me, and begun his move toward the door of my room. When he reached it he turned to me one more time.

"You were mean to her, very mean. Cruel, too. You should have brought her back." With that he put his right thumb under his front teeth and gave me the ultimate Italian gesture of disdain.

The next morning I told my doctors about this adventure and asked if they might find the guy and remove him from my case. I presume they must have done something; fortunately, I never saw him again. However, for understandable reasons I'm still cautious about Tebaldi's New York fans, even to this day.

But I'm never cautious about my feelings for this extraordinary artist, whose legacy is gloriously captured by her recordings. Having heard her in person during her brilliant years and knowing the unchanging magnificence of her recorded work, Renata Tebaldi, like Birgit Nilsson, will always be symbolic to me of the best in opera's modern golden age.

Joan Sutherland

❧❧❧

I did not know Joan Sutherland until I joined the Metropolitan Opera in 1971, and when she and her husband, Richard Bonynge, and I first met, our relationship did not exactly get off to a promising start. I was well aware that the talents of this rare artistic team had allowed Sir Rudolf Bing to revive some of the great bel canto operas of Bellini and Donizetti, much to the delight of the operagoing public and the box office, but I also knew Goeran Gentele was not a Sutherland aficionado and had no particular plans for her when he took over the company.

I strongly disagreed with his feelings, making it clear I thought the New York public—and for that matter the United States public—would not understand such a decision. As a consequence he invited me to be present when he had his first official meeting with them.

That conversation had not been under way five minutes before Bonynge realized there were no future plans to discuss. Very politely he reminded his wife of another engagement. Both arose from their chairs at the same time and were out the door before anything further could be said. I followed them to the corridor, hastily explaining that Gentele had only just arrived in New York and needed a little time to examine the workings of his new company.

Bonynge turned to me and said, "He can take his time. There are other theaters that will continue to make us welcome."

We shook hands. I said I knew things would work out in the long run if only they would not make too many hasty decisions at this particular moment.

"Perhaps the three of us might meet in the next days and discuss specifics," I suggested. "The Metropolitan would not be the Metropolitan without you both."

"We'll see," he replied, just as the elevator was arriving, and then, turning, added, "After all, we both love the New York public."

I telephoned Gentele and reiterated that the Met without Sutherland was an impossibility. I reminded him that one of the reasons I agreed to join his new management was to keep him on the straight and narrow regarding New York's cultural realities and that an offer to the Bonynges had to be made with some dispatch.

"Oh, all right," he answered, without much enthusiasm, "do what you can."

Shortly after this conversation the three of us met at the Bonynges' Brooklyn apartment. Joan and Richard were understandably put out by what they regarded as the general manager's indifference; their coolness was hardly subtle. I arrived to find Joan sitting on a couch with an enormous needlepoint project spread over her lap. She was wearing glasses, over which she would occasionally peer at me as Richard and I talked. Unlike other artists who often, in awkward positions, revert to raising voices or banging tables, these two were icy calm. We went over a lot of ground; I was sweating because I could not visualize our new management starting off by alienating this important operatic team.

As it happened the Bonynges were already scheduled in our first season for two productions, *La Fille du Régiment* and *Rigoletto,* a season that because of operatic time warp had, in large measure, been prepared by the Bing management. They also knew that a new production of *Les Contes d'Hoffmann* had been penciled in for them for the 1973–1974 season; no plans had been made beyond that point.

I started my arguments by picking up on their comments about the New York public and somehow found a way to suggest there were compelling reasons for appearing every season. I talked about their recordings and the need to promote them on a regular and uninterrupted basis. I sensed both had shrewd business heads but thought it might be uncouth of me to mention this fact in too brutal a fashion. I avoided the direct approach by pointing out the tenors: Pavarotti, scheduled to sing in both *La Fille du Régiment* and *Rigoletto,* was often a recording partner; the upcoming *Les Contes d'Hoffmann* would bring her together with Domingo. I suggested London Records, their recording company, was certainly not going to overlook the delightful circumstances of bringing several of its most important artists together in New York at the same time; I pulled every argument I could muster out of my somewhat nerve-racked operatic grab bag.

Finally I stopped talking; they both smiled. They knew the arguments made sense and quickly agreed to the *Hoffmann* for the 1973–1974 season, as well as accepting the suggestion we talk about 1974–1975 and 1975–1976 in a few weeks.

Joan Sutherland's first performance for the new management was a reprise of her triumph from Bing's final season, Donizetti's magnificent romp *La Fille du Régiment.* This opera, which caused Hector Berlioz, in a sharp phrase, to exclaim that Donizetti was treating France "as a conquered country," had first been an enormous success for her when she sang it at Covent Garden in 1966. At that time she encouraged the management to engage a new, young Italian tenor as her costar. His name was Luciano Pavarotti; the two were reunited in the Metropolitan production, together with Sandro Sequi, the young Italian who directed the work at Covent Garden. Ljuba Welitsch, a great favorite of New York audiences in earlier years, was cast in the colorful nonsinging role of the Duchess of Crakenthorp.

It is often said about theater that comedies are the harshest and trickiest works to perform, and if that's true—and I fervently believe it is—then comedic operas obviously lead the theatrical pack. One has only to think about the ghastly performances of supposedly amusing works cluttering up the opera stages of the world to realize the truth of this observation, and no one was more aware of this than Joan Sutherland.

Sutherland approached the revival as if she were starting all over again. Working with Sequi to reblock all the stage business, she insisted on careful and complete musical and stage preparations with the entire cast; she was leaving nothing to chance.

DAME JOAN SUTHERLAND

Brooklyn, New York
December 11, 1986

I photographed Dame Joan two days before she sang her silver anniversary performance with the Met. Knowing that on stage she would be presented the traditional silver tray, Dame Joan, in her inimitable Australian accent, joked: "Now I can officially be proclaimed an old dame." I jumped in, simulated holding a mike, and, taking on the air of a reporter, asked: "Dame Joan, as you now approach this momentous occasion in your career, what advice do you have for young singers?"—the oft-asked and mundane question. With her salty humor, Dame Joan was quick to reply: "To all aspiring opera singers I would say, 'Hasten slowly!'"　　　　**—J.D.R.**

Since this was my first professional association with her, I attended a number of rehearsals, watching as she set about helping Sequi and her husband bring order and discipline to the piece. She obviously enjoyed working with the cast, but her most demanding time had to be spent with Pavarotti, since she shared many of the opera's key scenes with him.

As I watched the proceedings I was struck by the curious fact that while both Sutherland and Pavarotti are large people, and give a first impression of being ungainly, they are, in fact, extraordinarily supple. As Sequi would set a bit of stage business, they would often stretch what he suggested to see how it physically fit them and what they might add with their bodies to punctuate the comedy and the music. At no time were they trying for burlesque; they were seeking perfect comedic timing with the care of professional vaudevillians and they didn't care how long it took to get things right. Often they would look at Bonynge for his reaction; they wanted all the pieces, after juggling, shaping, and discarding, to have his final approval.

One "piece," however, had special problems. As I mentioned earlier, Bing had engaged Ljuba Welitsch, the Bulgarian soprano who in one of his early seasons had jolted Metropolitan audiences with her ultrasexy Salome and bombastic Tosca, to play the

Duchess of Crakenthorp. Doubtless he did this out of compassion for a once-brilliant artist, and during his last season, when he was around, she behaved very well indeed.

However, with the new management it soon became evident she had lost none of her infamous eastern European temperament; at one point I felt it would be wise to have another artist on tap in case she and I came to a parting of the ways. I immediately thought of the striking actress Tammy Grimes, who I knew to be an opera fan and who I thought would love an opportunity to appear at the Metropolitan Opera as a member of the company. She had seen and loved the production and when I called her with the idea of joining the cast, she, quite literally, dropped the telephone.

"Darling," she whispered after recovering the instrument, "I could only be on that stage if I got the tenor. I need the final curtain with Pavarotti in my arms. That wouldn't work, would it?"

"No," I replied, "not in this opera, but you could make a grand entrance, coming down the big staircase with all eyes on you."

"I'll think about it," she answered, but after doing just that she turned me down. I decided to chance it out with Miss Welitsch, who eventually calmed enough to do a superb job.

At the January 6, 1973, premiere, all the separate pieces came together into a magnificent whole. The careful, painstaking rehearsals resulted in an afternoon of glorious singing and high comedy, with nary a ham bone in sight. Sutherland was brilliant, her voice cascading up and down Donizetti's score with laughing ease and her stage timing impeccable. Pavarotti, too, was at his considerable best and stopped the show with his nine high C's in the aria "Pour mon ame." The public adored every moment.

Shortly after this happy event the Bonynges agreed to stay with the Metropolitan, completing their 1972–1973 obligations with a stunning *Rigoletto* that again paired Joan and Luciano in the two principal roles. At the end of the season we all looked forward to the 1973–1974 production of *Les Contes d'Hoffmann.*

That particular physical production had been created for the Bonynges by the Seattle Opera in 1970, and we agreed to import it. From the standpoint of the Met's schedule it was to be treated as a new production, allowed the full rehearsal time needed for such a venture.

It's lucky we did. As it turned out, the sets and costumes barely survived the cross-country transportation. When unpacked they were in need of considerable repair and restoration. The truth is that what might have been acceptable in Seattle looked hideous on the Met's huge stage.

Joan quickly made it clear her costumes were to be remade by Barbara Mattera. I called the Metropolitan costume department to cope with the basically vulgar ensemble clothes, and the scenery department to redo the sets. Since both the designer, Allen Charles Klein, and the director, Bliss Hebert, were making their Met debuts with this production, they were extremely cooperative about our suggested changes, but I was still dismayed at the general tackiness of the whole venture.

Joan and Richard were also upset; I assured them I was as well. In a sense this production was a proving ground of just how much I wanted to cooperate with them. I made it clear to all my colleagues I expected miracles delivered with elegance and grace.

And that's what happened. On the opening night, November 29, 1973, the stage sparkled with lights and glamour; the sets, trimmed and repainted, looked more than acceptable; and the new and remade costumes were opulent. But most importantly, Joan was radiant, singing all the soprano roles in this difficult tour de force, brilliantly supported by her husband in the pit and her leading man, Placido Domingo, on stage. We had a triumph, and equally important, the Bonynges felt the Metropolitan's new management was genuinely concerned about keeping a strong relationship with them.

These new feelings all came to a test four weeks later when, on the morning of a scheduled *Hoffmann* performance, Richard called with the unhappy news that Joan was flat on her back with the flu.

"It's the first time this has happened in the twelve years we've been at the Metropolitan," he exclaimed. "Joan is beside herself with frustration. But since she cannot even sit up, her frustration is futile. I'll be in, of course, but you must call her cover. I can assure you she is prepared."

Somewhat wanly I asked whether there was a chance Joan might recover in time for the evening, but as I asked I realized the question was silly. As an Australian, Joan has, like most American artists, a sense of serious responsibility about her commitments, a quality often missing from some of her European colleagues. I was learning this fact in an unexpected way; I noticed the Italians, French, and Spanish of both sexes seemed quite casual about canceling, often basing their decisions on the recommendations of the late Dr. Wilbur J. Gould, a prominent New York throat specialist. As it happens, Dr. Gould removed the tonsils from three of our four sons and at the time we'd been impressed by his skill as a physician and his kindly attitude toward his patients. He called me, after I'd been appointed acting general manager, to wish me well and to warn me he would probably be calling quite a lot during the opera seasons.

"Sometimes there'll be medical problems," he said, "and sometimes there will be problems having nothing to do with throats. Since the artist will usually be sitting in my office when I call you, try to listen carefully to what I'm saying. Sometimes a good yell from you will be all I need."

No call from Dr. Gould was necessary this time. I began realizing, however, that I was going to undertake a task no other Metropolitan general manager had: announcing to a full house that Joan Sutherland would not be singing.

First, I reached Joan's understudy, the pert Canadian Colette Boky, who arrived in my office within minutes, flushed and excited, to assure me she knew all three parts and was ready to go on. A rehearsal was scheduled with the music and stage departments for early afternoon; I telephoned Bonynge to tell him the arrangements.

That only left the problem of informing the public, and to prepare for that ordeal I called Joan's sickroom. She was brought to the phone croaking and coughing but anxious to help in any way she could. Together we sketched out an announcement, essentially welcoming Miss Boky to her unexpected debut and suggesting that a bright, new talent was about to burst onto the opera world.

"You'll have to make that speech very carefully," observed Bonynge. "I don't envy you!"

I didn't envy myself either but, as some wag once commented: "When in Rome, wear a toga!"

As the audience arrived that night, they were greeted by signs placed all over the lobby announcing Sutherland's illness and the name of her replacement. I don't believe anyone really noticed them, but after the houselights had been lowered they certainly noticed the sickly yellow light illuminating the gold front curtain and the thin pencil microphone rising slowly from the stage floor. The light and the microphone were familiar signs: someone was coming out to make an announcement before the beginning of the performance, a moment always greeted with restless, unhappy anticipation, often punctured by loud cries of "Uh-oh."

When I stepped out they knew it was serious business. I lost no time in reading the message from Joan asking a warm welcome for Miss Boky. When I finished there was surprising applause, but as I was about to retire behind the house curtain, flushed with a kind of victory, one of the standees let out a loud "boo," followed by an unmistakable Bronx cheer. Others took up that theme, causing me to waste no time at all reaching the safety of backstage. As I did I heard another round of applause, and in seconds the applauders seemed to be drowning out the booers.

As I turned to walk down off the stage, I noticed four enormous stagehands, arms folded, two on each side of the curtain, looking at me.

"What are you fellows doing here?" I asked.

They looked at each other and finally one spoke.

"We're here to carry out your body," he said. "We were afraid the audience would kill you when they heard the news."

I thanked them for their concern and immediately retired to my box.

Miss Boky scored a nice success, singing extremely well. I was—and still am—grateful for her spunk and professionalism. Alas, she was not an overnight sensation. Except for a few hours after her performance, and a day or two of publicity, her career was never as exciting again. One always hopes in such situations for a magic rags-to-riches drama; I'm afraid that's more often fiction than fact. It certainly was this time, but nonetheless she saved the performance and prevented a wholesale audience revolt, no small accomplishment in itself.

Shortly after Joan recovered from the flu she and Richard came to my office to discuss a subject very much on their minds: over the years they had asked Bing to produce Bellini's *I Puritani;* it was a work Joan very much wanted to perform in New York. Bing always turned them down. How did I feel about this? I replied I thought it was a brilliant idea and would think further about it.

I didn't tell them I needed to discuss this particular opera with my colleagues because I knew Gentele had promised *I Puritani* to Beverly Sills for her long-overdue Metropolitan debut. I had a talk with Beverly herself who, when confronted with the problem, reacted with great understanding. She made it clear if some outside star were to debut at the New York City Opera, her company, with a work she cherished, she would never sing with the company again. She agreed we'd find another work for her first Met performances.

Within hours I called the Bonynges and confirmed we'd do *I Puritani* for them in the 1975–1976 season. We agreed on Sandro Sequi as the director and Ming Cho Lee as the designer.

"Try to get Pavarotti for Arturo," Richard suggested, "and Sherrill Milnes for Riccardo. I also suggest James Morris for Georgio. That will be a splendid cast. And thank you for working everything out."

"Thank Beverly Sills," I murmured to myself as I put down the phone.

In surprisingly short order we had all the pieces in place for this difficult opera, but I confess I had no idea how we were going to produce it. *I Puritani* is one of those works with gorgeous music but dreadful problems for the stage. It's full of entrances and exits of armies and individuals, as well as lots of static moments to allow singers full-range displays of vocal gymnastics, but dramatically it's a bore. I was worried about this aspect and stated my concerns to Sequi and Ming Cho Lee. Those problems were excitingly solved one morning by Ming, who arrived in my office clutching a handful of sketches.

"I know what we do!" he exclaimed. "We mask the stage with a great rendering of one of those gilt rococo frames that always surround a classic painting. We turn the whole piece into a series of such paintings: Rembrandts, the whole Flemish school. We pose the singers. We take advantage of the opera's static dramatic possibilities."

Sequi and I knew at once he was right and lost no time in suggesting to the Bonynges how we wanted to approach the opera. They were both enthusiastic.

Joan and Richard also had another suggestion. Since they were not going to be with the Met during the 1974–1975 season, what about two productions in 1975–1976? They had persuaded Kurt Adler, then general director of the San Francisco Opera, to stage Massenet's *Esclarmonde;* why didn't I come out and have a look at it? I'd never heard of *Esclarmonde* and wasn't about to display my ignorance. I did some hurried homework and discovered the opera was, apparently, the composer's favorite. It had been written for a soprano of prodigious vocal and sexual talents who also happened to be his mistress. It sounded promising. I flew out to San Francisco in October 1974 to see and hear it, and promptly placed it on the Met schedule for the winter of 1976.

RICHARD BONYNGE

Brooklyn, New York
December 11, 1986

"It's for posterity, Ricky!" Dame Joan teased as she switched places with him, Bonynge now in front of the camera. —J.D.R.

The decisions on *I Puritani* and *Esclarmonde* finally convinced the Bonynges I was serious about wanting to work with them, and in turn, this led them to make a difficult decision to participate in a major international event for the Metropolitan.

In the winter of 1973 I was approached by a young Japanese impresario, Kaziko Hillyer, inquiring if the Metropolitan would make a trip to Japan in 1975. The Chibbu-Nippon Company, a commercial television network based in Nagoya, wanted to celebrate twenty-five years of success by presenting the Metropolitan in Tokyo, Nagoya, and Osaka. They wanted three productions and a lot of stars, including Pavarotti, Corelli, Marilyn Horne, and Sutherland. I said I would see what I could do and began by approaching Sutherland.

At the mention of the word *Japan,* Joan's face froze. She looked over at Richard, her eyes wide and sad, and reached for his hand. He looked at her, smiling gently.

"I'm afraid that's difficult for us," he said quietly. "You see, Joan's brother was a Japanese prisoner of war and pretty badly mauled in the process."

I asked them to think about the trip anyway and let me know their decision as soon as possible.

It wasn't until the end of the 1973 spring tour, while the company was in Minneapolis, that I had the opportunity of bringing the matter up again. We talked in the Bonynges' hotel suite, and as with my first house visit to them, Joan had another large needlework project spread out on her lap. Richard told me they had both talked with her brother who urged them to visit Japan and let war problems fade into history.

"But it's going to cost the Met a lot of money!" he added.

And, indeed, it did. By the time we were through negotiating, I'd agreed to two of the largest fees in the Met's history up to that time, but as it turned out, every penny was earned.

The 1975 Japanese tour, the first successful foreign expedition ever undertaken by the company, opened in Tokyo with *La Traviata.* Joan was at her sparkling best but was only greeted politely by the audience. This was puzzling; her records were great favorites in Japan and she was making her debut in that music-loving country. It wasn't until the second act that we found out why.

The moment Robert Merrill, singing the elder Germont, made his entrance, the audience went wild, so much so that the performance had to be halted until the applause and bravos subsided. Merrill was almost panic-stricken; I happened to be backstage and he looked over at me wide-eyed while checking to see if, somehow, his trousers were unzipped. When calm was restored the act proceeded, but at its conclusion the storm started all over again. With the first curtain calls it became obvious the applause was not for Sutherland but for Merrill, and I had a moment of panic that the soprano was not going to be pleased at being upstaged by the baritone. I need not have worried. As soon as Sutherland realized what was really happening, she took him firmly by the arm and brought him to the front of the stage. When releasing his hand she gestured toward him and began to applaud herself, gracefully stepping into the wings as she did so.

Merrill continued to be bewildered by what was going on. After the fourth bow he told the stage manager he was heading for his dressing room and there he was joined by his wife and children, who were equally astonished. As it turned out, the Japanese had a long history of listening to him on pre- and postwar recordings and especially in the early fifties, when he performed regularly with Arturo Toscanini and the NBC Symphony during the maestro's concert performances of Verdi operas.

No one could have been more pleased with his recognition than Joan Sutherland, who shared the Merrill family happiness and often joined the stage-door fans by applauding when he left the theater. It wasn't as if she was ignored—there were plenty of her fans screaming and carrying on as well—but the emotional surge was for Merrill, and she sensed these were very special moments for him.

Joan and Richard are truly a collaborative couple and frequently speak of their work together as "our career." They tend to refer to Joan's voice as "the voice," as if it somehow belonged to both of them. The two have enjoyed parallel careers since 1962 when Richard began conducting for her, an exclusive alliance that some critics claim has restrained her reach. In a 1988 newspaper article under the rubric title "Joint Ownership," Richard had this to say:

> People say it would have been more widening of her horizons to have worked with other people. In the past Joan worked with everyone you could think of, but then she got to a certain stage where she was happy to be able to perform always with me. It saved her a great deal of effort, a great deal of time, and a great deal of friction. She's never been a vastly confident woman. She'll say "Oh, I couldn't sing that role," and I tend to have to persuade her a great deal to undertake many roles. The fact that we've been together for so long and the fact that I care about her voice means I've been able to help her look after it. I can hear the things

she thrives on and the things that don't do her good, and I try to push her in the right direction.

Joan herself points out that private conversation between them continues even in performances. "Sometimes just a look of the eyes or the raising of an eyebrow or his left index finger pointing skyward will tell me Richard thinks I sound a little bit flat."

Joan Sutherland, who formally retired from the opera stage in 1990, is that rare combination of enormous talent and extraordinary humanity. She knows who she is, and what position she occupies, but what is equally important to her is life outside of the music world. The partnership with her husband is a partnership on all matters, family as well as professional. Their only child, Adam, a successful businessman in the food and hotel management industry, has always been a major part of their lives. He's made them grandparents, new roles they both adore. There is a basic realness about both of them which I think springs from their Australian roots. They both have humor that is deep-seated and unharmful to others, plus a sense of fair play that comes out in all their dealings with people.

Richard and Joan revel in life and are not afraid to share their feelings with family, friends, colleagues, and the general public. Their place in the history of opera is firm and gleaming.

Eileen Farrell

Eileen Farrell, America's great dramatic soprano, was recently recognized as one of the few modern artists to fit the old, almost extinct Italian category of *soprano drammatica d'agilità*—literally an agile singer who can sing just about everything. This is a rare accolade, exemplified by Eileen and her colleagues Maria Callas and Joan Sutherland in our time and such past greats as Lilli Lehmann, Lillian Nordica, Elisabeth Rethberg, and Rosa Ponselle. Eileen's attitude toward such an appellation would probably be a shrug of her shoulders, a smiling laugh, and a throwaway line, for if there is one thing that defines this artist, it's an ability never to take herself too seriously. Don't misunderstand: she takes her work very seriously indeed. She just doesn't consider her career the be-all and end-all of her life. At the height of her powers she kept her schedules tautly arranged between time at home as a wife and mother and as little time as possible for professional obligations.

I really got to know this extraordinary woman in the 1960s, during my years as head of the Masterworks department at Columbia Records. There we recorded her singing a wide range of repertoire, including Wagner scenes, Verdi and Puccini arias and duets (often with the tenor Richard Tucker), French art songs, German lieder, and the songs of Cole Porter, Richard Rodgers, George Gershwin, Irving Berlin, and Harold Arlen. She was—is—the only dramatic soprano who could encompass such a variety of styles and forms and be totally at home in each. Early on we discovered we shared a number of things in common—a love of the variety of music, the same birthday, and the fun of lively families.

EILEEN FARRELL

Yarmouth, Maine
October 27, 1988

"One of my most unforgettable experiences in my career was at a rehearsal in the Mormon Tabernacle, with the Salt Lake City Symphony. The Tabernacle was empty except for the orchestra and myself, and we were doing Wagner's Immolation Scene from *Götterdämmerung*. It was an emotional experience that I shall never forget." Farrell's words seem to reflect the mood of this photograph. Who would ever suspect that jazz and rhythm and blues *blasted* through the stereo as we worked?   —J.D.R.

In those days she and her late husband, Robert Vincent Reagan, a retired New York City policeman, and their two children lived in a sprawling house on Staten Island in New York City. Occasionally, when our four boys and the Reagans' two kids were youngsters, we would spend a family day together that included a good deal of roughhousing and games. At one of these outings our son, Sam, then just learning to tell jokes, asked Eileen if she knew where a six hundred-pound canary would sit. She shook her head. "Anywhere it wants to," said Sam, grinning broadly. Eileen then got down on the floor and, bringing her face very close to Sam's, asked if he knew what a six hundred-pound canary would sound like. He shook his head. "Like this," she said,

and let out a high C that promptly had him—and the rest of us—covering our ears. We then sat down to one of the biggest suppers I've ever seen on any family table. She wasn't certain of our children's tastes and just to be safe prepared mountains of fried chicken and a huge roast of beef plus all the trimmings. I remember thinking our combined weight might sink the ferry on our ride home.

When Eileen's attention was focused on professional matters, she liked to work

with people she regarded as friends. One of her favorites was Leonard Bernstein, whom she affectionately referred to as Ben. For my money the two of them recorded the definitive version of Wagner's Wesendonck songs in a recording session with the New York Philharmonic that lasted an entire day. After they finished the songs, however, both suddenly realized they were also supposed to record the *Götterdammerung* Immolation Scene. "Don't worry, Ben," she said, "I'm ready. Let's go!" She loosened her dress collar, winked at the orchestra, and gave a nod to the maestro. At the end of the first take the orchestra cheered, as did everyone in the control room. "Ben" and Eileen embraced.

Unfortunately, other than the recording studio, the world of opera itself was almost always anathema to Eileen. She sang her first full operatic role on November 8, 1955, in New York's Town Hall, a concert performance of Luigi Cherubini's *Medea* with the American Opera Society. As a result of this performance the small world of critics and dedicated opera connoisseurs underwent a distinct tremor, much like winning the Kentucky Derby with a dark horse who'd never won a race before. Up to that time Eileen Farrell had been a very dark operatic horse indeed. When she stood on the Town Hall stage that unforgettable night, she displayed, in the words of one observer, as much animation as a totem pole, but when she opened her mouth there was no denying her singing; it was great by any standards. Through her voice alone, Cherubini's Greek heroine—a tragically maddened woman who murders her own children—emerged with astonishing theatrical realism and intensity of feeling. Farrell's voice seemed limitless in power, magnificent in tone, and remarkably sure in its command of classical style. The press exploded: Alfred Frankenstein of the *San Francisco Chronicle* wrote that "Eileen Farrell has a voice like some unparalleled phenomenon of nature. She is to singers what Niagara is to waterfalls."

The furor surrounding this performance came as something of a surprise to Farrell—both pleasant and unpleasant. She was understandably proud of her reception but a little resentful of the special fuss being made over what she regarded as just another job of singing. Since this was a craft she'd been pursuing for years, she did not fancy being a newcomer, however brilliant, who'd just been rescued from obscurity. Through a succession of programs presented over the years by CBS Radio—first a sustaining program called "Eileen Farrell Sings" and then programs commercially sponsored by such companies as Bayer aspirin, Coca-Cola, Chrysler Motors, and the Prudential Insurance Company—she'd been reaching a much larger audience than any theater could accommodate. She was as well known on Main Street as she was in the concert halls of the big cities. She'd been making quite a lot of money, too, and could certainly be regarded as a success. Under the circumstances, she was not inclined to be especially dazzled by the glittering new world of opera. "Glory be to Saint Patrick!" she was reported to have exclaimed to an interviewer after the Town Hall concert. "There's nothing difficult about singing *Medea.* You must pay attention to the words and do what comes naturally."

For ten years after her formal debut she allowed herself to try other operatic adventures, including a five-year contract with the Metropolitan, where she dutifully sang the Italian repertoire Rudolf Bing assigned her—*Nabucco, La Gioconda, Alceste, La Forza del Destino, Andrea Chenier* and *Cavalleria Rusticana,* operas that were easy for her but that made no demands on her formidable abilities. The Met public responded enthusiastically but also wrung their collective hands when roles that should have been assigned to Farrell—Wagner and bel canto parts—were ignored or given to others. When her Met contract expired in 1965, she shrugged her shoulders and pretty much disappeared from the opera scene, having never had the passionate devotion to a career that inspires most divas. Besides, she hated the Met, loathed Rudolf Bing, and contented herself, after her contract lapsed, with the occasional recital and remunerative appearances on television while collecting royalties on her numerous recordings.

Yet the memories of her successful appearances are still treasured by many operagoers. During the early 1970s, when I was in charge of the company, I tried to talk her into coming back. "No way, baby," she said several different times over a number of telephone calls. "I'll just stay home and listen to the broadcasts."

Teresa Stratas

At the start of the 1990–1991 season, as I heard Teresa Stratas once again on the stage of the Metropolitan in John Corigliano's *Ghosts of Versailles,* I was suddenly flooded with memories of years ago, memories mixed equally with frustration, exasperation, love, and awe at this slip of a woman whose gigantic talents always make audiences forget just how physically tiny she really is. Those talents are to be found not only in her voice, which has entranced opera audiences for over a third of a century, but also in her stage personality, which, like her looks, can sometimes recall a fascinating mixture of street-tough sexuality and pathetic vulnerability.

Watching and listening to her, I was immediately plunged back to my time at the house, recalling unforgettable experiences—her Nedda to Richard Tucker's Canio, in which, from the first moment to the last scene, she drove Tucker crazy enough to make him into the actor he never was; the dress rehearsal of *Otello* where, as Desdemona, she filled Jon Vickers with such passionate vulnerability that audiences were certain they'd make love right on stage even before the curtain closed on Act I; and her eerie versatility in portraying the three dissimilar heroines of Puccini's *Il Trittico*.

That Stratas is a great singer is beyond question. Barely five feet tall, slender, red-haired, and with the biggest, darkest eyes on the opera stage, she has, since her Met debut in 1959 at age twenty, played the most fragile of victims and toughest of tough cookies—Liu, Mimi, Desdemona, Nedda, Lisa in *Queen of Spades* on the one side; Lulu, Salome (in a film), Offenbach's brassy Perichole, Jenny in *Mahagonny* on the other. And Melisande, who fits into both catagories. "My voice," she has said, "is an extension of my soul." In her private life, where her childhood was out of the darkest Dickens novel, she has suffered debilitating bouts of misery. "I'm basically," she once told an interviewer, "a very introverted person living a very public life."

Stratas is a lyric soprano with the vocal agility of a coloratura, and has a powerful enough voice to be fully capable of filling large auditoriums. She has an enormous range and is an excellent musician and, disdaining coaches, learns all her roles by herself. Above everything else, she has that mysterious quality known as "presence"—the ability to demand attention the minute she appears onstage. It's a quality once shared with another North American of Greek origin, Maria Callas.

That said, I also think back to the times when this great artist gave me more than my share of managerial heartburn. The first was within days of Gentele's death, when she withdrew from his *Carmen* production where she was to have sung Michaela. I was looking forward to hearing her in this role, which is usually played for its cloying sweetness but has within it the potential of a strong woman once-too-often scorned. I knew there had been interpretive conversations along those lines with Gentele himself, and probably musical ones with Bernstein as well, before she accepted the role, but almost immediately after Gentele's death, and without even so much as a telephone call, I received indirect word she'd canceled. I tried reaching her but to no avail.

When we finally did meet during rehearsals for *I Pagliacci,* however, all thoughts of betrayal disappeared as I watched her shape Nedda into a character specifically designed to seduce Richard Tucker the man as well as Canio the character. It was her way of getting

TERESA STRATAS

New York City
June 9, 1992

She avoids the trappings of glamour, shunning publicity and the frills of the profession: to Stratas, her art is just one facet in her quest to serve, public acclaim an intrusion. And so, one day, Stratas, with only a backpack, travels to India. She finds Mother Teresa and asks to be of service in the Home for the Dying. Stratas is a private person, and I felt privileged that she allowed me to intrude her world with my camera. In front of the lens she was reticent; but when she began to play peekaboo with the dog, I was able to capture a seldom-seen aspect of her personality.

—J.D.R.

him to forget about acting and draw from him the scattered passions I think she correctly surmised lived, boiling, just below the surface of his life. I have no idea whether they actually had an affair, but I do know that onstage she made Tucker give the most electrifying performances of his life, leaving audiences stunned and shaken.

But with Stratas, you never knew from one minute to the next whether your feet were on the ground or on banana peels.

I'll never forget the scheduled season premiere of *Otello* I mentioned earlier. The first performance was a 2:00 P.M. Saturday-matinee broadcast, and at about 11:00 A.M. Stratas called to cancel. Her cover was a new one to the Met who was scheduled to take on the role after Terry (as she is affectionately called) completed the first three performances. Fortunately the cover had thoroughly rehearsed the role in proper anticipation of what we all felt was

going to be a major Met debut, but I didn't know whether I'd find her at home on this particularly lovely fall morning.

I didn't. When her apartment phone was finally answered by her husband, he told me his wife was out taking a long walk with their dog and was not expected back for at least an hour. I asked if there was any way of reaching her. "I'm afraid you'll just have to wait," he said. "Is something up?" I took a deep breath and told him it would be necessary for her to make her Metropolitan debut this afternoon. He seemed unfazed and said she'd call me the minute she returned. I left him my private number.

I alerted my colleagues to the cast change, telling the artistic administrator to be in touch with the second cover (yes, we actually had two, a caution learned over the years of dealing with Stratas). At 12:15 P.M. my special phone rang and I explained the situation. The cover said she'd come to the theater immediately. I then called Vickers to alert him to the change; he took the news in his stride.

By 1:30 P.M., when I made my customary half-hour-before-the-performance visit to all the members of the company, I knocked on Desdemona's dressing room door to wish her well. She was sitting calmly, dressed for the first act and having the final touches put on her wig and makeup. "*Toi-toi* for this afternoon," I said, "and the best of everything. Sorry your debut has to be so hurried." "Oh, that's all right," she said, giving me a warm smile, "it's my job." I leaned down and kissed her.

A few minutes before 2:00, I announced to the audience that we were sorry Teresa Stratas was ill but I hoped everyone would be pleased by the unexpected debut of Kiri Te Kanawa. They were pleased, in both the front and back of the house, to such an extent that at the close of the last act, Vickers took her out for their bows together and stepped back, applauding, to let her be on the stage alone. The applause and cheers were deafening.

Later that afternoon, Stratas called to tell me how magnificent Kiri had been and to wish her well for the future.

Which is also something we all wish for Terry—this waif of grand talent who is one of the finest singing actresses on any stage today. We cross our fingers, always waiting for her next burst of excitement.

Dorothy Kirsten

I fell hopelessly in love with the late Dorothy Kirsten in the 1940s, initially hearing her on the radio and then seeing her onstage at the Metropolitan Opera. I first discovered her special magic during a Met broadcast of Massenet's *Manon,* which she quickly followed with several other radio appearances as a singer of popular songs teamed with her friend Frank Sinatra. The fact that she could grab your ears and wring your heart playing one of opera's tragic heroines, and do the same with popular music, put her in a category shared only with Eileen Farrell. Like Farrell, there was always a sparkle in Kirsten's voice, an invitation to share the joy in whatever she performed that was, at the same time, uniquely professional and unmistakably American.

We first met in the early 1950s, during the last years of Edward Johnson's tenure as the Metropolitan's general manager. At that time I began playing a minor role in her concert activities, working with her manager, Frederick Schang, and occasionally escorting her to various concert dates. She was a joy to be around, but during those days I never dreamed we'd work together except in my role as a junior tour assistant. Actually we

didn't—until I was unexpectedly propelled into the post of the Met's general manager.

As pointed out by Lanfranco Rasponi in his delightful book *The Last Prima Donnas,* Dorothy Kirsten's career followed a very special pattern. With the exception of a year spent in Italy, she was entirely trained in America. Born in New Jersey, the daughter of a builder and church organist, she studied voice with the idea of going on Broadway and took classes in what she described as "aesthetic dancing" with one of the original Mary Wigman dancers.

It was actually a radio program that opened her horizons. The Metropolitan's glamorous soprano Grace Moore happened to hear her and sought out the young soprano, arranging for her to go to Italy to further her studies with Maestro Astolfo Pescia. Italy was a huge success; Maestro Pescia was not. In Kirsten's own words:

> He wanted to turn me into a dramatic soprano but I knew my own voice better than he did. When I returned home I went to Ludwig Fabri and took classes with him until he died at the age of ninety-three. With him I sang Mozart over and over again, although I never did it on the stage, for I didn't have the type of instrument needed for his music. But his arias and songs were my training ground. I discovered a singer is much like an automobile. If you drive in town a lot and shift gears constantly, your car will last far less

DOROTHY KIRSTEN

Pacific Palisades, California
November 5, 1991

Having suffered a stroke, Kirsten did not wish to be photographed; yet with persuasion on the part of her secretary and confidante Vicki Hillebrand, she finally acquiesced and a date was set for me to photograph her at her home on the West Coast. I flew out from New York, only to learn on arrival that Kirsten had reconsidered and would not sit. Vicki intervened, daily trying to coax Kirsten on my behalf and telephoning me each morning with the prospects, as I remained on the Coast for what stretched into a duration of two weeks. The third week I sent white roses. Kirsten telephoned, and with trepidation agreed to a sitting. I promised my camera would be kind. —J.D.R.

time than if you drive it mainly in the country. If you jump from one repertoire to another, the way most singers do today, the voices inevitably suffer, like the gears.

Dorothy Kirsten had a very distinguished career and won deserved international fame even though she only appeared twice outside of the United States: once, in the fifties, on a tour that included performances in Moscow, Leningrad, Tiflis (now Tbilisi), Riga, and Stockholm; and in 1975, during my tenure at the Met, on the company's first tour of Japan, where she sang Mimi in Tokyo, Nagoya, and Osaka partnered by Corelli and Pavarotti. She sang for more consecutive seasons than any other leading soprano at the Metropolitan—thirty years—and built her tremendous following with relatively few roles. She knew how to husband her resources with keen intelligence and shrewdness.

She officially retired from the Metropolitan on December 31, 1975, at age fifty-six after a gala *Tosca,* but occasionally sang opera again when desperately needed to replace an indisposed colleague. In 1979, for example, at age sixty, she came once more to the rescue of a Met *Tosca* by flying in from California at the eleventh hour to replace Leonie Rysanek, who had suddenly been forced to cancel. I say "once more" because in the spring of 1975, just prior to the Japanese tour, she flew in to save a *Tosca* on a non-subscription Saturday night, and anyone present at that extraordinary performance will never forget it.

That night I should have sensed an operatic disaster brewing after leaving her calm and orderly dressing room and moving on to that of her Cavaradossi for the evening, Franco Corelli. Here I found the tenor in a tantrum, railing furiously over some obscure Italian political matter he'd been arguing about with the evening's conductor, Carlo Felice Cillario. He was, quite literally, shaking with rage. When I left his room I naively thought his display of extra energy might spice up the performance. It never crossed my mind that political disagreements would become the evening's artistic focus, with conductor and tenor scoring musical points off each other for the entire performance. Matters reached a melodramatic climax in the third act, when Cillario refused to wait for the applause after

Corelli's *"E lucevan le stelle,"* and the tenor, furious, put his thumb to his teeth and ran off the stage. That left the audience stunned, the orchestra still playing the ascending scale leading to Tosca's entrance, and Tosca herself bursting onto the stage to find it empty and the audience buzzing around in a minor uproar. Until Corelli was pushed back onto the stage to resume his role, Kirsten had to sing all their love music to herself, a unique experience for any soprano. She was more amazed and amused than angry.

Dorothy Kirsten was fortunate never to be plagued by illnesses. From the very beginning she knew how to look after herself, limiting her engagements and leading a healthy outdoor life in California and Hawaii. The performances she canceled during her long career were few and far between; she earned the eternal gratitude of American impresarios.

She also knew the commercial importance of the Metropolitan. She needed its name for her recitals, which always brought her much greater income than her operatic roles. She was a good recitalist in the grand tradition. People expected a diva and they got one, always in an effective, becoming gown, properly bejeweled and impeccably groomed. She gave audiences far from highbrow programs, but she didn't sing down to them either. She always managed to find a happy medium and the public adored her. Her many radio, and later television, appearances helped her build a name throughout the United States. She never played important parts in movies, but she benefited enormously from the publicity of those she did do. She could have done more in the movies, but Sir Rudolf Bing didn't much approve of that sort of thing.

When she began her operatic career she specialized in a French repertoire— Manon, Gounod's Juliette, Marguerite, and Gustav Charpentier's Louise, a role she studied with the composer himself. She told Rasponi that the old man was "charm personified and used to having English and American girls coming and begging for his advice." However, despite her impressive credentials with this part, she could never get Bing to revive it for her. "Instead he offered me Marie in *Wozzeck,*" she said, "and I turned him down."

Despite her disappointment over *Louise,* she and Bing had mutual respect for each other, a respect that ended up with his offering her roles she was happy to undertake.

Those included her greatest Italian opera successes—Butterfly, Mimi, Tosca, Manon Lescaut, and Minnie.

By the time I arrived at the Met, Dorothy Kirsten had settled on singing only these Puccini roles, and she did them with consummate artistry. She would have a few scheduled performances each season but made it abundantly clear I was to call on her first when emergencies arose with operas in her repertoire. This I often did, usually reaching her at a country club as her indomitable assistant would always leave word to find her on the links if a call came from the Met. Often there would be very little time between my call and the need for her to show up in New York. Of course, I never tried her when the emergency was an afternoon cancellation for that evening's performance, but occasionally an artist would ask for an advance release, which I might grant if Dorothy was free and willing to come.

That is, in fact, how she joined the Japanese tour in 1975. Ten days before the tour began, Renata Scotto, scheduled to sing Mimi, was forced to withdraw, leaving the Met in the dreadful position of having impeccable casts for *La Bohème* but no star Mimi. I called Dorothy, reaching her on the golf course and proposing that she take over the role. She'd already told me she was planning to retire from the Met at the end of 1975 and that maybe the Japan trip, a strenuous undertaking at best, was a little too much. We discussed the pros and cons, and then suddenly I told her I was desperate. "One more trip before your gala *Tosca* farewell," I pleaded. "We really need you." There was a brief pause. "Right," she said. "I've got it. The Met's in trouble. I'll be there."

And she was, charming the public in her handsome way and discovering the Japanese were longtime fans of hers from recordings, broadcasts, and films. She sang with Corelli—long forgiven for his *Tosca* tantrum—and Pavarotti alternating as her Rodolfo, bringing her formal Metropolitan Opera career to a glorious close.

Magda Olivero

A Hall of Fame for Opera might one day be created by singers themselves, and if such an institution were to happen, there's no doubt in my mind that one name would occupy a prominent spot on almost everyone's list of nominees for membership: the soprano Magda Olivero.

Olivero, an artist now at least in her late seventies and still singing—she posed for the pictures in this book in early 1992, after completing concerts in Milan—finally made her Metropolitan Opera debut in 1975. That she should have been ignored by previous Met managements is one of those operatic mysteries that cannot be untangled. Obviously she failed to pass muster with Gatti-Casazza in the late thirties, Edward Johnson in the forties and early fifties, and Sir Rudolf Bing from the midfifties until his retirement in 1972. She might have been overlooked by me as well if it hadn't been for a last-minute need to find a substitute Tosca and a scheduled lunch with Marilyn Horne.

Horne and I were lunching to discuss a production of *Le Prophete* for her in the 1976–1977 season, but as our food arrived she suddenly asked what I was going to do

about the Tosca performances recently vacated by Birgit Nilsson. I told her Nilsson had given up the role in order to sing Sieglinde opposite Jon Vickers's Siegmund, and I hadn't as yet come to grips with this particular end-of-season problem. I did tell her I wanted to find someone who would stir up a lot of interest and not be viewed as a pale substitute for a leading prima donna, but at the moment I had no idea who that might be.

"I do," she said, picking up her fork, "and I heard her sing the role in Dallas two weeks ago. She was sensational."

"Who are you talking about?" I asked.

"Magda Olivero," she answered.

"Magda Olivero?" I replied. "But she's got to be in her mid- to late sixties. How could she possibly sing and act Tosca?"

With that Horne took off on such a complete critical analysis of the lady's style and technique that I was drawn to listen to every word. After lunch I mulled over what she'd said, made a few calls to check her story, and then came myself to the startling realization that Olivero's appearances in the New York area had almost always been confined to Newark,

MAGDA OLIVERO

Milan, Italy
January 29, 1992

She was Ciléa's favorite Adriana. I found Olivero one of the gentlest and most sensitive artists I've encountered—without ego, but with a rare ability to totally abandon herself in front of the lens and evoke passion.   —J.D.R.

New Jersey, the home of the New Jersey Opera. She'd often sung there, as well as elsewhere in the United States and throughout Europe, including La Scala, the Florence Maggio and Comunale, Rome, Paris, Berlin, and the Edinburgh Festival, where she'd offered a wide repertoire of Italian, French, and German roles, many of which had been recorded for Decca. But she'd never set foot on the stage of the Metropolitan.

Olivero's fascinating career goes back a very long time. Hers was—is—a small voice produced in such an expert manner that she could always be heard in large theaters over large orchestras. The Italians have an expression for this phenomenon—*"voci che corrono"* (voices that run). She was a mistress of that technique as well as *"l'accento,"* the articulation of words which in many instances can be made to substitute for a lack of vocal power. When dramatic passages demanded a big sound, Olivero, by her intelligent and able phrasing, always worked miracles to create the atmosphere of a grand crescendo. She was also a stunning actress.

I found she lived in Spain and cabled to ask if she might be free in early April to sing Tosca at the Met, with James King as her Cavaradossi and Ingvar Wixell as Scarpia. Her reply was gracious: yes, she was free and interested, but could I tell her how much rehearsal time was possible? I cabled back she could have as many room rehearsals as she required, but that there would not be time for any rehearsals with orchestra or on the stage itself. There was a pause in our communications after this news, but within a few days she wired again that she understood our situation and would be delighted to come.

Her first day in the theater was unforgettable. Bodo Igesz, the house director responsible for staging *Tosca,* came to me almost in tears about what an actress she was and how she was going to be deeply moving in the role. Shortly thereafter Jan Behr, who was doing the musical preparation, came to my office to say the same thing. They were both stunned by Olivero's artistry, and you can believe this information quickly spread all over the house.

It also spread to the general public. Tickets for her performances were quickly sold out, and I began receiving the occasional letter congratulating me. It was all a kind of guarded approval for my decision to replace Nilsson with this greatly loved soprano who had heretofore been denied the Met.

On the night of April 3, 1975, Olivero took New York by storm. At her entrance there was a spontaneous explosion during which she waited, completely in character, for the audience to quiet down. She then took up her part with controlled passion and palpable tension. King and Wixell, having worked hard with her in room rehearsals, knew exactly what she—and they—were going to do. The result was a first act of equal parts love and horror. I've seen Toscas recoil from their first confrontation with Scarpia, but none with such restraint, dignity, and obvious loathing.

In the second act she threw herself on a couch before singing *"Vissi d'arte,"* and when she finished you could see her change from despair to cleverness to an assassin, every

moment moving like an unwinding spring. As she placed the candles around Scarpia's corpse you knew she was a woman in total command of her surroundings.

At the end of the third act, when she realized she been tricked by the firing squad and that Cavaradossi was dead, her leap over the parapet brought gasps from the audience.

When the curtain came down, the audience rose to their feet. The curtain calls went on for half an hour, during which time both King and Wixell brought her forward to the edge of the stage and stepped back to join in the ovation. She had a total triumph, and at long last had made her debut at the Metropolitan Opera.

The soprano Maria Laurenti, who often sang with Olivero until she herself took early retirement, was asked whether she thought Olivero should retire. I like her comment:

> I think there is a time for every artist to take stock and know when to retreat gracefully. There are rare exceptions such as Magda Olivero. She is a phenomenon apart. Once when she was delivering some pianissimos that were out of some other world, I asked her where they came from, for the thought crossed my mind that they were head tones. Not at all. She took my hand and put it over her diaphragm, and it was more solid than a rock. No one knows her exact age, but I don't think it matters. What does is the fact that with the thread of a shattered voice, she can hold an audience in the palm of her hand. That is art.

Presenting this great lady was one of the special pleasures of my years at the Metropolitan.

Leontyne Price

Leontyne Price has filled many a hall and ravished many an ear since her first performances as Gershwin's Bess in 1953 and 1954—or even earlier in a Juilliard School *Falstaff,* where the seeds of her Verdi repertoire were sown. Those who heard her then knew she was destined for the top, and soon came that procession of international triumphs: San Francisco, Chicago, Vienna, London, Salzburg, the Metropolitan, and La Scala—indeed, she triumphed everywhere she appeared.

I was first privileged to hear Leontyne Price in the postwar 1940s, at the home of Florence Page Kimball, her mentor, teacher, vocal advisor, and friend. I don't remember the exact date, but I do remember it was shortly after my wife and I were married. Florence—or Auntie Flo, as she liked to be called—was a friend of both our families and the widow of a gentleman named Schuyler Smith; as a consequence, she fully approved of my first name. She also seemed to approve of me, since she knew I was passionate about music and just starting to find my own niche in the music world. She thought we ought to hear her star pupil, and included my wife and me as guests at what she liked to call one of her "little blue plate suppers."

From that moment, which absolutely stunned us both, to this writing, I have been privileged to know Leontyne Price. Simply put, she is one of the glories of America, as a woman, an artist, and a human being. From time to time I've had the pleasure of working with her, starting almost at the beginning of her concert career and continuing, off and on, during my time at the Metropolitan Opera. Ironically, our time at the Met turned out to be the last years of her major New York operatic activity. She is, in the parlance of the day, "some piece of work!" or, to put it in slightly more dignified terms, she is, alongside William Faulkner and Eudora Welty, Mississippi's greatest cultural gift to world civilization.

There were five people in the story of Leontyne's life who were crucial to her development, and they all lived in the little Mississippi town of Laurel, where she was born and named Mary Leontyne Violet Price. Her mother, Katherine Price, was a strong, proud woman who taught her daughter the art of getting along in a white-dominated world and, in later life, became a midwife and pillar of Laurel's black community; her father, James Anthony Price, was a quiet, reflective man who earned a living as a carpenter; and third was a favorite aunt, known to the family as "Big Auntie," who followed Leontyne's development with avid interest and worked as a maid in the home of a white couple named Chisholm.

The Prices lived on Laurel's South Fifth Avenue, a dirt road that ran as far north as Magnolia Street, where it suddenly changed into North Fifth Avenue, a paved street where white families lived. The Alexander Chisholms lived on North Fifth Avenue. Mr. Chisholm, a northerner from Vermont, made a lot of money in Laurel, from lumber, oil, and banking. He and his wife often helped Laurel's younger people, both black and white, get on in life. The Chisholms, people of excellent intentions, were of assistance to Leontyne. But a myth, which might be called the "Chisholm legend," grew, largely because it made good newspaper copy. It was said that the Chisholms were responsible for her career, and this error has distressed both Leontyne and the Chisholms.

The fact of the matter is that Leontyne's father and mother worked hard, mortgaging their home to support their daughter's early musical training and later to send her and her brother, George, to college. Leontyne once told the late Winthrop Sargeant that "I had musical palpitations ever since I was four and everybody, especially Mama, thought I was some kind of a musical prodigy." She studied the piano with Hattie V. J. McKenna, a local teacher, and before long was playing the piano in Laurel's black Methodist church. She is still a good pianist, playing occasionally for friends.

The Price family was very close. "I did not know we were poor," she remembers. "My family was affluent in love, deep religious background, respect for our fellow man, affection, faith, and simplicity—a hell of a combination. My mother was a part of the community, always available to every problem."

Katherine Price was also an educated woman, having attended Rust College at Holly Springs, just outside Memphis, when it was only a one-building campus for blacks. She insisted her daughter get an even better education, sending her to Central State College at Wilberforce, Ohio, which was then a black school. On graduation Leontyne received a certificate allowing her to teach music in the public schools. Her ambitions were already beyond that, but it was something to fall back on in case of need.

What first stimulated these ambitions was a concert given by Marian Anderson in Jackson, to which her mother had taken her when she was a little girl. "I was nine and a half," Leontyne recalls, "when I first heard Marian Anderson. It was just a vision of elegance and nobility. It was one of the most enthralling, marvelous experiences I've ever had. I can't tell you how inspired I was to do something even similar to what she was doing. That was what you might call the original kickoff."

Later, at Central State College near Xenia, Ohio, she had another experience of almost equal importance. Central State is close to Antioch College, and the choirs of the two colleges often got together to sing oratorios. Paul Robeson, the great black baritone, visited Antioch to do some lecturing and singing, and at his recital there he invited Leontyne to sing part of the program with him, giving her a portion of the receipts. She saved this money, augmenting it by working at the college cafeteria. On graduation, she made straight for New York, where she got a scholarship at the Juilliard School. The already-mentioned Florence Page Kimball, a Juilliard teacher, took her under her wing and became her guide, vocal coach, and friend until the day Kimball died.

My professional association with Leontyne Price began with her now-famous 1954 audition for Herbert von Karajan, which took place late one fall afternoon at Carnegie Hall. At the urging of impresario Walter Legge and concert manager André Mertens,

LEONTYNE PRICE

New York City
July 31, 1986

"Do you want my *Leontyne* look or my *Miss Price* look? This is my Leontyne look"—an exaggerated smile—"and this is my Miss Price look"—suddenly the haughty diva. "How about just *Leontyne Price*?" I asked.   —J.D.R.

Karajan agreed to hear her, and became so enthused that he bounded out of his seat and onto the stage where, after a few admonitions, he eased her accompanist (the incomparable David Garvey, who is still her accompanist) aside and began to play for her. Later that same afternoon, at a meeting between Mertens, Legge, and myself, Karajan made it clear he would make her a world star if, from here on in, he had first call on her European activities. This was agreed upon, and the upshot was a long association between them, beginning with an appearance as Pamina in *Die Zauberflöte* at the Vienna State Opera, then her first engagements at La Scala and the Salzburg Festival, and continuing until the conductor's death.

By the time Leontyne Price arrived at the Metropolitan in 1961, she was well prepared. It's unusual for any singer to do five roles in a first season at the Met, but she had been familiar to audiences in New York, Chicago, San Francisco, and various European (and even Asian) cities for quite some time before her Met invitation. Her actual American operatic stage debut took place at the San Francisco Opera in 1957, where she was engaged for a small role in Poulenc's *Dialogues of the Carmelites*. She soon was given the leading role of the Chief Prioress, and when Antonietta Stella, who was to have sung Aïda, took ill with appendicitis, she took over the role in her place, doing it for the first time.

Throughout her career she always maintained a real affection for the San Francisco

Opera. The late Kurt Herbert Adler, then the opera's able general director, advised her not to make her debut at the Met until she had a number of roles under her belt and not to type herself by first appearing in the black role of Aïda. She followed his advice.

It's not surprising under the circumstances that her 1961 debut at the Met was made with considerable assurance. She was solidly prepared to take on the Verdi and Puccini roles as well as the Mozart operas; her musicianship was virtually faultless.

It was five years later, at one of the peaks of her career, that the Metropolitan opened its new home at Lincoln Center. Bing commissioned Samuel Barber to write an appropriate work to mark the occasion. Barber chose Shakespeare's *Antony and Cleopatra* and persuaded Bing that Leontyne would be the perfect Cleopatra. The adapter of the Shakespeare text, as well as the director and designer of the sets and costumes for the production, was Franco Zeffirelli. The production was a disaster.

Zeffirelli overstaged the opera to the point where Barber's splendid music was scarcely noticeable. His scenic arrangements turned out to be a nightmare for everyone—a moving sphinx as big as a locomotive that broke the Met's new turntable; a golden pyramid in the center of the stage that refused to open for Leontyne's entrance, requiring her to crawl out in a costume and headdress that made her look more like Medusa than Cleopatra. Nothing was right.

The experience gave her a permanent dislike of Zeffirelli's work; she vowed never to sing again in one of his productions. On the other hand, like any prima donna, she did insist on a new production from time to time. "It's not exactly a thrill to go up to Sixty-third Street and do the same old Aïda," she remarked.

Shortly after the calamitous opening, Bing offered her a new production of *Il Trovatore.* She was delighted until she heard Zeffirelli was to design and direct. She put her foot down. She would not sing under those circumstances. Bing fell back on Attillo Colonello, whose designs were even worse than Zeffirelli's. Leontyne dutifully sang this production, but she was getting fed up with Bing's designers. The following season she did not sing at the Met at all. "Mr. Bing was livid with anger when I told him I was not going to sing that season, but that was that. I had made up my mind." The season after that she sang only four performances of *La Forza del Destino.* Meanwhile, she had sung two solid months at the San Francisco Opera. "After all, that's where I made my first debut," she explained.

In the fall of 1971, when Goeran Gentele and I arrived at the Met, Leontyne's relationship with the company was distant. Gentele immediately offered her a new production of *Don Giovanni,* making it clear this was to be the first of a series of exciting projects he had in mind for her. Before any of his ideas could be discussed, however, he was killed and I became acting general manager.

One of the first things I did in this new post was telephone Leontyne and ask for a meeting. She was sympathetic to my position but made it extremely clear she could live happily without the Met. "But the Met can't live happily without you," I countered. "You and I have been friends for a long time. Can't we at least talk about the future?" After a pause she agreed. We made a lunch date for the following week at one of her favorite New York restaurants, La Côte Basque.

La Côte Basque is famed in song and story as chic, power oriented, and expensive. In those days it was presided over by Madame Henriette, a conservative French woman who was extremely fussy about her clients' clothes, especially her female clients'. When Leontyne arrived with a dark mink coat covering elegant black pants, Madame Henriette rushed to my table to inform me that La Côte Basque forbade women in pants.

"Madame," I said, mustering all my dignity, "if you deny Leontyne Price, I'll never be able to persuade her to return to the Metropolitan Opera. She asked to lunch at your restaurant. Please! We need her back on the Met stage. New York misses her. Help me!"

She looked long and hard and then broke into a smile. "Never let it be said that La Côte Basque denied our city a great artist," she said. "I say rules can be bent. I bring her to you myself!"

On arrival Leontyne seemed slightly bemused by the seeming intimacy between the proprietress and myself. *"Bonne chance, Monsieur Chapin,"* Madame Henriette murmured while pulling out Leontyne's chair. *"Vive l'art. Vive New York. Vive Leontyne Price!"*

The lunch was delicious, but we took a long while to get around to business. She was already scheduled to sing a few performances of *La Forza del Destino* in 1972 and then nothing until Gentele's new *Don Giovanni* in 1974. I asked her if she would consider *Madama Butterfly* in 1973 and *Manon Lescaut* in 1975. She was reluctant to give me answers. We talked about my wife; about Florence Page Kimball, who was then painfully ill; about her work with Karajan. But she smiled, ducked, and weaved when I pressed her on Met matters. Finally she said she'd think about the *Butterfly*s for 1973 and might also consider the *Lescaut*s for 1975, even the old Met production dating back to the fifties, if I engaged our mutual friend and her old colleague, Peter Herman Adler, to conduct for her. (In the late forties and early fifties, Adler had been chief conductor and artistic director of the NBC Opera, the only opera company ever created exclusively for television. He'd spotted Leontyne early on, giving her many opportunities to sing her first major roles.) I gulped. On my recommendation Gentele had engaged Adler to conduct *Un Ballo in Maschera;* the results had not been happy, especially with the orchestra. "No Maestro Adler, no me," she said in a quiet but definite manner. I gulped again.

Several days later she called, saying she would sing two performances of *Butterfly* at the beginning of the 1973–1974 season if we settled on Adler as conductor for the *Lescaut*s in 1975. It wasn't as much as I wanted, but considering her feelings about the Metropolitan Opera, I was grateful she'd agreed to anything at all.

Then, a few weeks later, I had to call and ask if she would come to my office to discuss a matter that had become urgent.

During my early weeks in the general manager's chair, I'd discovered the real depths of the Met's financial problems, which had been a shadow background during Gentele's first days. I now had to make a decision to cancel one of his scheduled new productions, and the most obvious was *Don Giovanni,* since I could always fall back on the Met's classic Eugene Berman designs, even if the production itself was in a disgraceful state of disrepair. There were others who would also have to be notified about this decision—Sherrill Milnes, who was singing the Don for the first time in his career, and Karl Boehm, the conductor—but to me the key player was Leontyne.

When she arrived at my office I took a deep breath and launched into the problem; she was, as always, a thorough professional. I explained we would keep the already-scheduled extra rehearsal time just as if it were a new production, and added I had high hopes of finding a special gift to pay for a complete rehabilitation of the Berman sets and costumes. She asked to be relieved of her last two contracted performances and insisted on new costumes but otherwise understood my problem and agreed to my request that she remain in the cast. She gave me a big hug before leaving the office and, smiling, looked into my eyes. "Some job you've got," she said, "but don't let it get you down!" I told her I'd do my best.

Thanks to Robert Tobin, an avid collector of Berman drawings, paintings, and artifacts, the old production was completely restored. When it appeared in the spring of 1974 it looked bandbox new and was a triumph for all concerned, with the single exception of Karl Boehm, the scheduled conductor, who had canceled. Boehm took personal umbrage at what he considered the scraping of *"his* new production." I was sorry about his decision, but good sometimes comes along with all the problems: I offered the opera to James Levine, who accepted at once and with it had his first Mozart opera success.

As promised, during the first week of the 1973–1974 season, Leontyne appeared in two performances of *Madama Butterfly,* but not before some heartfelt agony. Florence Page Kimball, after two ghastly strokes, was now confined to her bed and the occasional wheelchair. Obviously a dying woman, she wanted desperately to be present for Leontyne's first performance, but since this was not going to be physically possible, Leontyne suggested—and I agreed—that we set up an extra onstage orchestra/singers rehearsal especially for her. Unfortunately, scheduling problems made it impossible for that rehearsal to take place on the *Butterfly* set. Instead it had to be done in the first-act trappings of *La Forza del Destino;* understandably, Leontyne was not too happy about this, and neither was I. However, there was little either of us could do if Florence was going to have her heart's wish.

And she did. I wheeled her into my box, clearing away the other chairs to make her as comfortable as possible. When Leontyne made her entrance Florence grabbed my hand and, with tears streaming down her cheeks, watched and listened as Leontyne sang only for her. It was a moment neither of us will ever forget.

My last project with Leontyne Price was *Manon Lescaut,* and while the orchestra did complain to me about Adler, I reminded them that his presence at the Met meant hers as well, an increasingly rare and special occurrence in those days. The players assured me they would behave themselves and they did. Leontyne was scheduled to sing the first three of six scheduled performances, but when her alternate showed up to rehearse for the remaining three, she turned out to be absolutely hopeless. How this happened I still to this day don't know, but I quickly called Dorothy Kirsten, who agreed to fly in from California for the fifth and sixth performances. That meant the fourth would have to be canceled unless I could persuade Leontyne to sing one more time.

With not a little trepidation, I called to ask this special favor. There was a long moment of silence on the telephone before she said she would, and on the fourth night I came before the curtain to announce that the posted artist was unable to be with us and the substitute would be Leontyne Price. The theater exploded with pleasure.

Alas, she doesn't sing staged opera anymore, but the concert halls of the world still explode with pleasure every time she steps out to sing a recital. Not long ago someone asked her how it felt to arrive at that moment in life when one is given the accolade of "national monument." She laughed with typical heartiness and replied, "I just want to burst out singing!"

That's what she's been doing now for over forty years, much to the delight of the world. She is one of those rare people—a joy giver. Her joy is contagious. We in the audience are the lucky receivers.

Beverly Sills

The haunting pictures illustrating this essay show a modern American legend—the girl from Brooklyn who conquered her world by combining considerable talent with a love of people and an almost unique ability to share her joys while onstage, in the recording studio, or on television. Exuberant, enthusiastic, effervescent, her outside happiness, while genuine enough, also concealed a shrewd mind, common sense, realism about the unreliable world of show business, and a family life pummeled by tragedy. One of my proudest moments with this grand lady was the night of April 7, 1975, when, at long last, she made her Metropolitan Opera debut.

Her debut vehicle was the difficult, pyrotechnical role of Pamira in Rossini's *The Siege of Corinth,* the same work that in 1969 shot her into international stardom at La Scala. It was the idea of her mentor, Edgar Vincent, to repeat this success at the Metropolitan after it became obvious that I had to withdraw Goeran Gentele's original offer of Bellini's *I Puritani* because of a potential conflict with Joan Sutherland.

Edgar suggested I reunite Sills with conductor Thomas Schippers and her La Scala costars Marilyn Horne and Justino Diaz, using the original Nicola Benois production designs and inviting the director Sandro Sequi to restage the work, thus showing the New York public exactly what had set La Scala on its collective ear. I thought this an excellent idea and decided to proceed. Marilyn Horne, whose international career had also been helped by the La Scala production, declined to repeat her role of Neocle because she was no longer going to sing "pants parts," the operatic term for girls playing boys. I offered the role to Shirley Verrett, who accepted with alacrity.

The rest, as they say, is history. Rarely has such an event been heralded with as much media attention. Beverly herself wrote in her charming 1976 autobiography *Bubbles*:

> I could not open a magazine or a newspaper without seeing my picture. I was welcomed at the Met like a long-lost child. Schuyler Chapin, who had taken over the Met when Mr. Gentele was killed in an automobile accident in 1972, fulfilled every promise that Mr. Gentele made to me. During a break in one rehearsal, when Shirley Verrett, Justino Diaz, and I were alone on the stage, I muttered that I certainly hoped we could live up to all the hoopla that was being made over this. "How can we miss?" Justino said. "I'm Puerto Rican, Shirley is black, and you're a Jew. We've cornered the market on minorities. Who would *dare* criticize us?"

She went on to write about that night, including her preperformance routine:

> When I leave home for the opera house to get ready for a performance, Peter [her husband, Peter Greenough] always says "Have a good time." I reply, "I'll probably sing like a pig." That opening night at the Met I found on my dressing table when I arrived a gift from Peter—a little gold pig from Tiffany's, mounted on a chain. Outside the Metropolitan, Lincoln Center Plaza looked, my mother said, like St. Peter's Square on

Easter Sunday. When I made my first entrance on the stage to sing my opening line, *"Che mai sento?"* (What do I hear?), I heard nothing but a tremendous roar from the audience. After my first aria the applause lasted so long that I got teary-eyed and had to walk upstage to compose myself. The curtain calls at the end of the opera were seemingly unending.

When all was said and done, however, the Met was only the maraschino cherry on top of a rich singing career, a career she decided to close out five years later in a gala evening at the New York City Opera, her operatic home base. But disappear from the opera scene? Not at all: at the time of her Met debut, she was already thinking about working on the other side of the footlights. "I've spent most of my life in an opera company," she observed. "I know the runnings and could be helpful." She was, too, and in 1980 became general director of the New York City Opera at a critical point in that company's history. For ten years she administered, handled casting, negotiated with the unions, auditioned, shepherded, and encouraged—and raised the money to keep the organization afloat. By 1990 she was ready to turn everything over to her successor, Christopher Keene.

In my opinion, during her singing days Beverly Sills was the greatest actress on the operatic stage, and that includes even the fabled Maria Callas. The quality of her voice and her enormous sensitivity to different emotions expressed in the varying tones of that voice were extraordinary, to say nothing about her enunciation of languages. Her French was superb—every word in an opera like

BEVERLY SILLS

*New York City
January 6, 1992*

I photographed Sills in a cramped corner of her living room because of a lamp. This highly amused her. Not that the apartment overlooking Central Park lacked atmosphere, but the turn-of-the-century lamp with its glass globes intrigued me: it seemed to evoke *The Ballad of Baby Doe,* the opera I most equate with Sills. Silent in front of my camera, Sills had a tendency to turn inward, and as I focused on her face I observed a sadness in her eyes—a direct contrast to the ebullient and vivacious personality she projects on stage and television.
—J.D.R.

Manon could be heard; likewise, her Italian was impeccable. When she brought the trio of Donizetti's Elizabethan operas—*Maria Stuarda, Roberto Devereux,* and *Anna Bolena*—to the stage, these showpieces for coloratura sopranos became ringing dramas. She even, from time to time, deliberately made her voice ugly in order to express fury or despair, in order to add drama to her performance. She was a rarity—an intellectual singer, approaching her work with a thorough grasp of historical subject matter and a clear idea of exactly what she was going to do. She could move an audience to tears with no apparent effort at all and bring it back to laughter in the same way.

As it happens, my wife Betty and I began our personal friendship with Beverly Sills when she married her husband, Peter Greenough. Greenough, Harvard class of 1939 and a college roommate of Betty's first cousin, Howland Davis, is a longtime friend of the New York/New England Davis clan. The Davises are a large, energetic, affectionate group who, after Peter and Beverly's marriage, welcomed her with unbridled enthusiasm. This relationship made it easier for me when I took up the details of her Met debut, but it proved especially helpful when the time came to organize the first operatic foray into the People's Republic of China.

A word of explanation: In the fall of 1976, having left the Met, I became dean of the School of the Arts at Columbia University, where, in 1978, because of the efforts of my colleague Chou Wen-chung, Chinese-born composer and vice-dean of the school, we established the Center for United States/China Arts Exchange. By 1981 the Chinese were rebuilding their music schools and sent word they would be honored if Beverly Sills would come to hear some of their students and lecture on opera in the west.

I approached Beverly with this idea and we turned the trip into a family affair—she agreed to go provided Peter, their daughter Muffy, and my wife and I were also to be included. She turned down a suggestion to do individual teaching in favor of master classes, as well as lectures which the two of us could do together, explaining the present systems for running opera organizations in the United States and Europe.

The Chinese were delighted, and on a hot, dry June afternoon we all found ourselves being welcomed at the Beijing airport by two extraordinary women who turned out

to be our "handlers," an older one named Lao Yu (literally "older" Yu) and a younger translator simply known as Kitty.

With Lao Yu and Kitty in command, we visited music schools and theaters in Beijing and Shanghai and throughout the provinces, where we were welcomed as conquering heroes. However, Beverly's first master class almost proved our undoing.

A group of eager singing students had been assembled at the Beijing Conservatory for the occasion, most having had only the skimpiest training. What little they had came from pre-1958 phonograph records supplemented by faded hand copies of operatic scores. As one after another took center stage, it was obvious a few had real talent but all had little or no sense of what they were doing. In order to demonstrate some technical points about breathing, Beverly went onstage, placing her hand firmly at the top of a young baritone's diaphragm. The entire audience gasped; Lao Yu's eyes went to the top of her head, her hand covering her mouth as Kitty rushed over, quickly explaining that in China intimate public touching between men and women was simply never done. We all looked at each other as Beverly explained to the head of the school that there was no other way she could be helpful if she was not permitted to physically demonstrate important points she was making. Lao Yu, Kitty, and the school authorities went into nervous conference, finally agreeing to make an announcement to the audience that what she was doing was professional, not a sexual invitation. I thought the baritone looked a little disappointed.

The high point of the trip, however, occurred in Shanghai, at a school with the odd name of Shanghai Philharmonic. There, an extraordinarily tall and handsome young tenor burst onto the stage with a "come hither" look rivaling Franco Corelli's. Beverly and I glanced at each other in startled amazement as he began *"Recondita armonia di bellezze diverse"* from *Tosca* with authority, a commanding voice and presence. Unfortunately by the time he reached *"L'arte nel suo mistero,"* the rest of the aria disappeared in confusion; he didn't know it. All he knew was the first part, having learned it on a collective farm from an old scratchy recording. He had impressed his collective leaders sufficiently that they pooled their resources to send him for serious study. A young peasant, literally just off the farm, he had arrived at the school a few days before our visit and somehow talked his way into singing for us.

Unfazed by having to stop, he started the aria a second time and fell apart at the exact same spot. Without waiting he immediately came up, smiling and full of personality, to make it clear he was ready for the opera world. The next thing we knew he'd maneuvered himself into a position to be photographed with Beverly, at the same time insisting we should take charge of his career. After he finally withdrew we all agreed that somehow he was going to make his mark on the stage and in the process add a new Asian dimension to the grand Yiddish word *chutzpah.*

Beverly Sills is herself a confessed workaholic. "It comes from my father who died when I was twenty," she once reminisced. "My mother gave us the dream. My father had energy and a good strong temper. He was a joyful man. My younger brother has it—he and I are the movers." Her accomplishments have brought pride to the girl who once knew hard times, who met a good deal of opposition and disinterest, who worked and climbed with true grit, who at a crucial time in her life used singing as an escape from personal tragedies, who learned to sing for pure pleasure and not just to build a career, and who probably never dreamed of the kind of wealth and réclame she has amassed from her superstar career.

Beverly Sills, who in one way or another over the years broke all the so-called rules of the game, remains today a glorious woman, a loyal friend, a loving wife and mother, and a unique American creation.

Sundry Sopranos, a Contralto, and a Mezzo

{decorative flourish}

During our work together, my collaborator, James Radiches, kept a small collection of photographs always just out of my reach. From time to time I'd ask to see them; from time to time he'd let me look, but never for very long. One day, however, he put the pile in front of me and asked what I thought about including these artists in our efforts.

The picture on top was Licia Albanese, an old friend, and as I looked at her photograph I was reminded that on opening nights of a new Met season or at a Metropolitan Opera Guild benefit or a special gala performance that's to be preceded by the national anthem, you're apt to hear Licia's voice cutting through the mush of audience singing—clear, commanding, bell-like—almost a clarion call to honor. These days she's a devoted member of the operagoing public, a splendid former prima donna of the Italian repertoire, remembered by old-timers as the frailest Mimi, the tenderest Butterfly, and perhaps the most haunting of modern Violettas.

Unlike many retired prima donnas, however, Licia is as bouncy and energetic as ever, deeply committed to an active life, with projects ranging from the health and security of older musicians to the discovery and nurturing of young talents to the state of Italian-Americans in general. Now a widow, she was married for many years to Joseph A. Gimma, an investment counselor and broker involved in New York State Republican politics. Gimma, one of New York's deputy racing commissioners, always relished the shiny state medallion fastened to the license plate of their car, allowing him to park any time on nearly every city street.

Joe and Licia were also deeply committed to the charitable work of the Archdiocese of New York, and she still is, as is their only child, Joseph, Jr., known affectionately as Pippino, a successful New York entrepreneur.

Licia is a shrewd judge of people, street smart and totally devoted to music, an art in which she's had an important role for almost fifty years. She has sharp ears, hearing through young singers to spot their weaknesses, encouraging them when she hears real talent, realistic when she doesn't.

I think it's also safe to say that Licia Albanese has never deliberately hurt anyone in her entire life, even while active in a profession known both for its beauty and its bitchiness. She rises above all the nonsense, bringing a lot of pleasure to the people she knows, including those of us who serve with her as fellow trustees of the Bagby Foundation for the Musical Arts, an organization devoted to caring for destitute musicians and encouraging youngsters of talent. She also cooks some of the best pasta I've ever eaten.

Next time you're at a Metropolitan gala, listen for that special voice floating over the house. It's enough to make you salute.

Another artist and friend whose photograph was in Radiches's collection was the beautiful—*regal* is perhaps a better word—Anna Moffo, who had a brilliant but too-brief career as one of the most effective singing actresses to grace the major opera houses of the world. I first met her in the early 1950s, when I was a young music manager working for the late William Judd. Judd first discovered her in Philadelphia and was confident that he had a major talent on his hands.

He brought her to New York to sing for a group of us, and I was spellbound by her strong lyric coloratura as well as her uncanny command of the stage. I remember at that audition she was wearing a dark green dress with a splash of red around her throat, and stood easily on the tiny stage of the Steinway Hall auditorium, where, by magic, she became Mimi, Butterfly, Manon, and Gilda.

In the beginning, her career moves were judicious, reaching a major point in 1959 when she took the Met by storm as a sensuous and passionate Violetta. It was easy to cry when she lay dying, the beautiful young woman crushed before her time.

LICIA ALBANESE

New York City
April 22, 1986

"*Povera Butterfly*" (poor Butterfly), they sing. But not Albanese! It was as Butterfly that she launched her career in Europe, and as Butter-fly that she debuted at the Met and at the San Francisco Opera. Albanese's credo? Butterfly's line, "*Io seguo il mio destino e piena d'umiltà.*" (Wherever Fate will lead me I follow willingly.) To Albanese, happiness is a butterfly . . . *Madama Butterfly*! **—J.D.R.**

When I arrived at the Met, however, Anna's singing was more frequently heard in the RCA Victor recording studios than on the stage. She was under a long-term contract to that company and had recently become involved with the company's chairman at that time, Robert Sarnoff. In the midfifties, Sarnoff and I worked together on the national tours of the NBC Opera Company. I knew he liked opera in a mild way, but it did come as a surprise when I began seeing him at all of Anna's Met performances. He was, of course, secretly courting her.

From my standpoint the love affair was crowned one night in the middle of a performance. Anna claimed sudden throat problems and disappeared; I had to send for her cover. The postscript to this story is simple: they married.

Anna now teaches and coaches, still sings the occasional performance, and looks as stunning as ever. She can be heard in a wide variety of roles on her RCA recordings, but I think first and foremost she is happy to be Mrs. Robert Sarnoff.

I sifted through a few more photographs and suddenly came upon the late Marian Anderson. Very few performing artists of any age have been as remarkable,

not only as the most musical of contraltos but as a human being of quiet dignity, whose example of courage and purpose opened the way for her fellow African-Americans to pursue artistic careers in any direction in which their talents took them. Throughout countless international and domestic tours, including her 1938 recital at the Lincoln Memorial and her two seasons at the Metropolitan, she constantly reminded audiences of the grace of her artistry and the elegance of her person.

I first heard her at Carnegie Hall as a little boy, taken to an afternoon recital by my father's godmother, Mrs. R. Osgood Mason. Mrs. Mason, for the price of allegiance to her odd philosophy of equal artistic rights but not civil rights, helped support a number of native American and African-American artists during the 1920s and 1930s, one of whom was Marian Anderson.

After the performance, Godmother (as she required me to call her) and I went backstage. I was introduced to Miss Anderson, who looked at me gravely and, when Mrs. Mason's attention was elsewhere, very slowly winked.

Over the years I heard this incredible artist as often as possible when she appeared in New York, and as a consequence my wife and I made certain we were in the audience on the night of January 7, 1955, when she made her long-overdue Metropolitan Opera debut in *Un Ballo in Maschera*.

That debut grew out of a supper party the previous fall, where she happened to sit next to Rudolf Bing, who suggested she join the Met to sing Ulrica. Unfamiliar with the

ANNA MOFFO

New York City
June 1, 1986

With her instinct for drama and an ability to create mood, Anna Moffo is the ideal model. I can vividly recall a session with Moffo in which we revolved the photographs around a piece of fur—a boa. At one point she had rolled the fur around her wrists and looked at the camera demurely. "Now feel the warmth of the fur," I said as I started shooting. "It's reminiscent of . . . Mimi." *"Mimi?!"* she broke in, an incredulous and slightly perturbed expression on her face. "Mimi? I *hate* Mimi! Those simpering, sugary characters. We'll do something else." With that she unwound the boa, letting it drape over her wrist, and, very lightly, put her cheek to the fur, musing. She had now become Violetta—or was she supposed to be Manon?

—J.D.R.

role because she had never sung on an opera stage before, she went over it with her old friend the conductor Dimitri Mitropoulos. Together they decided this was the perfect role. Thus Marian Anderson, in her fifties, began to prepare for one of the supreme moments of her professional life. The Met, through Bing's decision, had finally opened a gate long closed—and with a singer whose conduct as an artist and a woman had been irreproachable.

The offer had come perhaps a little late in her artistic career, but she rose magnificently to the occasion, working with her fellow artists Zinka Milanov, Richard Tucker, Leonard Warren, and Roberta Peters, and conductor Mitropoulos, to give a remarkable performance. For her it was a soaring personal triumph. There were eight curtain calls. "Anderson! Anderson!" chanted the standees, and men and women in the audience wept. I was one of them.

Away from the pressure of public life, Marian Anderson was a lady of good cheer, quietly pleased that her career made it possible for her fellow African-Americans to work anywhere. She had a sly sense of humor about herself, keeping the public and private parts of her life quite separate. At one point several years ago, PBS asked me to do a television conversation with her and we met several times to discuss the project. I only wish I'd had a tape recorder on those occasions as she looked back at many of the incidents, adventures, and pleasures of a crowded life. Unfortunately we never came before the cameras. The money for the series dried up, to the horror of at least New York City's public television station. I was distressed. Marian Anderson was fatalistic. As always, I learned from her.

MARIAN ANDERSON

Danbury, Connecticut
May 16, 1990

Frail at ninety-three, Marian Anderson slowly made her way to the entrance hall, using a walker; there, she greeted me. As I watched her approach, she seemed to be encircled in light—a radiant light, an aura. In front of my camera, this most private woman, a shy woman, was humble. There was a sense of mission about her . . . a sense of calling. "I will lift up mine eyes unto the hills," her face seemed to say. Clearly she was one who heard the voice of the Lord.   —J.D.R.

BIDÚ SAYÃO

New York City, March 27, 1986

I had long admired Sayão's Columbia classic of Villa-Lobos's *Bachianas* No. 5, that I brought a cassette recorder to the session in the hopes that Sayão would recount the experience of making this historic recording. She did, and I transcribe her words verbatim, charming as they are in her English: "Villa-Lobos wrote that piece for eight cellos and a violin. And I heard this in Brazil, and I got in love with this beautiful melody, and ask him I want to sing. And he said, 'No. I wrote this for eight cellos and a violin. Is for *instruments,* not vocally.' I said, 'But I can *humming* imitate the violin. Always in my exercises I humming because it's good for the vocal cords.' And he said, 'Well, let's see when I'll be in New York. I going to think about, because is a piece that you must vocalize: we must put some words in between, and in the end you can humming or imitate the violin.' So I wait when he came here in New York; I visit him and we learn together. And after he says, 'I want to hear with the eight cellos. We go to the Columbia Records.' So we went to the studio. In that time it was very primitive: today, with new machineries, you can amplify, you can make a diminuendo, you can make a big voice small or vice versa . . . but in my time we have just one little microphone in front of me. And so he rehearsed with the cellos. Each cellos has different contratempo and they don't play the same thing. And so was hard. And after he said, 'Now we're going to put all together—we're going to make this rehearsal all together. Don't stop. If we make a little mistake, never mind. I want to see everything together how sounds. And in case, after, we repeat again until is beautiful done.' And I asked the engineer before I start, 'This is a very delicate piece, because in the end I must humming. And humming is very difficult—is accomplished when the mouth is shut, and the sound comes from the nose. And if you force that, you start to tremble and is very bad. It must be steady. And so what I going to do in the end?' He said, 'Well, you have the microphone and you approach or you go back a little bit. You doing your intuition. And after, we see the result.' So I did what I thought. And after that we went back to hear. And we heard and Villa-Lobos was very pleased: nobody made any mistake, the sound was good, and he said, 'I don't think we should repeat.' He asked the musicians, 'Are you happy?' They said yes. And he asked me, too! And I said, 'Well, if *you* like, Villa-Lobos, *I* like it. I think it comes out very nicely.' And so he asked the engineer, 'The first rehearsal, can it stay forever—to make the record?' He said, 'Certainly. If you want, sir.' And this is it. In six minutes—*six minutes*—we record a record that was best-seller for two years!"

—J.D.R.

Almost the next picture that caught my eye was the petite and enchanting Bidú Sayão, who during her career days held audiences in the palm of her hand, whether on the opera stage, the concert hall, a living room, or just in conversation. A tireless devotee of her Brazilian countryman, the composer Hector Villa-Lobos, she seized every opportunity to promote his music, probably doing more for him than any other artist of her time. At the Met, her clear, bright soprano and winning ways as an actress caught my imagination when I was a teenager and first heard her in 1937 as Mimi. I fell in love, but ran into headlong competition from my father, who'd lost his heart earlier that same year when she'd made her debut as Manon, the only opera he ever really liked.

REGINA RESNIK

New York City
April 26, 1986

Resnik's studio was divided by a pair of French doors that were painted white, glass and all. I saw them as flats on an opera stage, echoing the second act opening of Ciléa's *Adriana Lecouvreur*, one of the first operas I had attended as a kid in Boston, with Resnik herself as the Princess de Bouillon. —J.D.R.

I fantasized about this elusive butterfly for years, enjoying her in a variety of roles—Rosina, Zerlina, Norina, Violetta, Juliet, Melisande, Manon, Manon Lescaut, Susanna, and especially her incomparable Mimi. During the fifteen seasons she sang at the Met she was, hands down, one of the public favorites. When, during my time as general manager, we finally met, I was totally unprepared for her wry humor and saucy conversation. She is still an extremely attractive woman who flirts outrageously and makes the man she's with feel as if he's the only person in the world. Very, very good these days for the somewhat squashed male ego.

Continuing through Radiches's special cache of pictures I spotted another old friend, Regina Resnik. Regina, at an age when most singers have long since retired, is still an active life force on the musical theater scene. She made her debut at the Metropolitan fifty years ago, as a soprano in 1944, and redebuted in 1956 as a mezzo, the voice range she settled into for most of her international career.

I first heard her right after World War II in soprano roles—Donna Anna, Tosca,

Leonore, Cio-Cio San—and then lost track until she reappeared at the Met in 1956 as Marina in *Boris Godunov* and then *Carmen,* a role that reestablished her as a singer and actress of considerable power.

Over my years in music management she and I developed a friendly professional relationship, meeting from time to time on the occasional project, but it wasn't until 1972 that we really worked together. It was on a revival of one of her favorite roles: the Countess in Tchaikovsky's *Queen of Spades.*

Like many other stars, Regina was in a state of shock after Goeran Gentele's death, coming to see me immediately to express concern over her immediate production problems but more curious about me, the relative stranger to international operatic intrigue. She was polite, a bit tense, and obviously skeptical about my ability to run the Metropolitan. I sympathized with her; I was skeptical myself. Somehow during that conversation we developed a strong rapport, perhaps because we were both native New Yorkers ready to face any crisis, but also because she sensed I cared a great deal about the Metropolitan and was prepared to do battle for things I wanted to accomplish.

Onstage that year her Countess was spectacular. She commanded the production, creating an unforgettable performance both within the context of the libretto and by using the Tchaikovsky score as a wrapping for character development. I knew she'd succeeded when my colleague, Rolf Liebermann, then intendant of the Paris Opera, told me what a success I had with *Queen of Spades* and congratulated me on overcoming all manner of obstacles to become a leading impresario. Regina was pleased when I told her of my "triumph."

After I left the Met, our professional paths did not cross again until 1988, when as a member of the Tony nominating committee I had the pleasure of voting for her as best featured actress in a revival of *Cabaret,* and in 1991 I again marveled at her talents when she played Madame Armfeldt in the New York City Opera production of Sondheim's *A Little Night Music.* Also in 1991 I spoke at ceremonies at New York's Hunter College, from which she graduated in 1942, when they conferred on her the degree of Doctor of Humane Letters, *honoris causa,* for the "intelligence and passion" that underlie her artistry and has "enabled audiences to know . . . the greatest aspirations, tragedies, and joys of the human soul. . . ."

A little hyperbolic, perhaps, but not too far off the mark. Regina Resnik is a life force that shows no sign of diminishing. Good thing. She keeps us on our toes.

Moving along through Radiches's startlingly brilliant photographs, I came across one of the late Jarmila Novotná, the beautiful Czech soprano for whom the Metropolitan Opera was only one distinguished chapter in an international career that spanned over thirty years. Beginning with her singing lessons in Prague with Emmy Destinn (she was too young to be accepted by the local conservatory), Novotná was associated with the most important between-the-wars personalities in the worlds of theater, opera, and film. Max Reinhardt staged *La Belle Helene* and *Les Contes d'Hoffmann* for her. Franz Lehar composed *Giuditta* for her to sing opposite Richard Tauber. At the Salzburg Festival her conductors were Felix Weingartner, Arturo Toscanini, and Bruno Walter. A film star in Germany, France, and America, Novotná is best remembered here for *The Search,* directed by Fred Zinnemann, with Montgomery Clift, and as a reigning star of the Met from 1940 until her retirement in 1956.

I first met her in 1944, when as a newly minted pilot in the Army Air Corps, I was home in New York on a brief leave. I was taken to the Metropolitan on a Saturday afternoon to hear her as Octavian and then invited to sit next to her at a dinner party being given for her by my aunt and uncle, Eleanor and Chester Burden. It was a wonderful moment for me.

At the Met, Novotná alternated the most glamorous roles with trouser parts, singing Cherubino in *Le Nozze di Figaro* more often than anyone in Met history, and Orlovsky in *Die Fledermaus* thirty-seven times, including her final performance on January 15, 1956.

She was introduced to the Met by Arturo Toscanini, who brought her to this country in 1939 to sing *La Traviata* with him at the New York Worlds Fair and had to cancel the performances because the hall at the fairgrounds bordered the runways of La Guardia Airport. "Since I called you here, I'll take you to the Metropolitan," he said, and promptly marched her down to meet the general manager, Edward Johnson. This in itself was extraordinary, for Toscanini swore he'd never have anything to do with the Metropolitan after he quit in 1915. He greeted Johnson by announcing *"Lei e un stupido!"* (You're a dummy!) Johnson said: "Come now, Maestro, what have I done?" "Well, why didn't you invite this Novotná a long time ago?" Johnson replied that his predecessor had but that she hadn't wanted to come. Another invitation was promptly issued and she made her Met debut on January 5, 1940, in *La Bohème* opposite Jussi Bjoerling, with whom she'd sung the role in Vienna. The rest is wonderful operatic history.

In 1989, to mark the fiftieth anniversary of her Met debut, John W. Freeman interviewed her for *Opera News,* where it became obvious that Novotná's busy life was still rich in family, friends, and music. "Of course there are many important things in life besides music," she was quoted as saying, "but that doesn't make music unimportant. If you love music, what would life be without it—can you imagine? Art is really what brings beauty into life. Look at the young people, always listening to music—different from ours, but it's music. Even if you just hear a little bit of a bird's singing, it's something lovely."

JARMILA NOVOTNÁ

New York City
December 5, 1991

The picture was taken two months after Novotná had been decorated with the Order of Tomáš Garrigue Masaryk, Czechoslovakia's highest civilian honor. We spoke of her homeland, and with emotion she recounted her coming to America: "I arrived in America, fifteenth of March 1939, and the horrible thing was that it was just the day when Hitler marched to Prague. I had been so anxious to see the Statue of Liberty—I came by boat, and all the while as we were out I thought, 'I will see now this most important landmark of America.' I didn't see anything: when they told me that Czechoslovakia had been taken by the Germans, I had only tears in my eyes." I found an alluring mystique in Novotná's face, heightened by her ability to underplay in front of the camera. —J.D.R.

I was continually captivated by this gracious, elegant woman, who exerted a magnetism over me that I remember to this day and which has characterized her throughout her long and eventful career. Until her death in 1994 she continued to be a lively presence in New York's musical life. She will truly be missed.

Right under Novotná's photograph I found Risë Stevens, who perhaps more than any other singer at the Metropolitan introduced mass audiences to opera and in the process became a household name, for a time almost synonymous with the word *opera*. She did this, of course, with her voice and personality on the stage, over the radio, and on phonograph records, but her special niche was her success in the movies—so great a success that at one point in the midforties a battle arose between Risë and her husband, Walter Surovy, on one side and MGM mogul Louis B. Mayer on the other. Mayer wanted more films; Risë, despite her film contract, wanted to return to opera. She won.

RISË STEVENS

New York City
May 15, 1986

By her own admission, Gluck's Orfeo was her favorite role, though the public frenzy was her Carmen or Dalila. "I know I was sexy on stage," she said, winking, at my telling her unabashedly that as a kid I used to treasure her recording of *Samson et Dalila*, thinking her voice the sexiest sound on record. I asked her to lean against the portal and look directly at the lens. As I focused in, she arched a brow, and Stevens became, through the slightest gesture, the seductress audiences remembered.   —J.D.R.

Risë Stevens actually made two debuts with the Met, the first, November 22, 1938, as Octavian in Philadelphia, and the second, December 17, 1938, as Mignon, her official "house" debut and a Saturday-matinee radio broadcast. In addition to these, her roles ranged from Orfeo to Dalila, but probably her most famous was Carmen, which she sang for 124 performances, the last on April 12, 1961, when she retired from the Met after a grand total of 348 performances.

But it was not just her work on the Met stage, or any of the other world opera houses in which she performed, that gave her a special place in American affections. It was the movies that took her from her position as opera star to mass entertainer and back again without in any way diminishing her artistic standards.

To the fans of classic movies, she is the star who sang with Nelson Eddy in *The Chocolate Soldier* and with Bing Crosby in *Going My Way,* among others. More people have heard her sing the Habanera from *Carmen* in *Going My Way* than heard all 124

performances she gave at the Met, plus all the others at La Scala, the Vienna Staatsoper, and elsewhere.

Stevens's singing career actually began in 1936 and it continued until the summer of 1964, when in response to the entreaties of Richard Rodgers, William Schuman, and myself, she closed out her active stage life with the role of Anna in *The King and I* for the Music Theatre of Lincoln Center. Just prior to that project, while I was still at Columbia Records, I persuaded her to record the Kurt Weill–Moss Hart musical *Lady in the Dark* for the Columbia Record Club, since no cast recording of that show had ever been made. It is curious that her last two performing projects were both parts that had originally been created by the late Gertrude Lawrence, the English actress who in her gutsy and compelling way was like Risë—a performing artist of marked power.

Over the years, Risë kept a nonsinging connection with the Met, where, over time, some of her offstage experiences turned out to be as fully dramatic as any she'd ever sung. In 1965, a year after *The King and I*, the Metropolitan Opera National Company was established to let young American singers begin substantial careers without going to Europe. Risë was invited to become codirector for the artistic side of this venture, which had the backing of the Met board president, the late Anthony Bliss, but the enmity of the general manager.

Bing wanted no part of the project and fought tooth and nail to prevent its success. However, he flew to Indianapolis to see the company's first performance, Carlisle Floyd's *Susannah,* and was apparently overwhelmed. In the elevator afterward he told Risë and Walter that it was one of the greatest performances of any opera he'd ever heard. "The kiss of death," murmured Walter when Bing got off. It was. The company struggled for two years and then the Met board refused an offer of major funding for the third—Bliss lost; Bing won.

Following the demise of the national company, Risë moved on to become president of the Mannes College of Music, where I served on her board of trustees, and then in the early eighties to become advisor to the Met's Young Artist Development Program, a position she held until 1988, when she was named to the Met Opera board as a managing director.

All one has to do these days is see her inviting smile to know that the French were right when they coined the phrase *"Plus ça change, plus c'est la même chose"*—the more things change, the more they stay the same.

The photograph that surprised me the most in Radiches's packet was, oddly enough, of Zinka Milanov, for twenty-nine years a star on the Metropolitan Opera stage and for another twenty-three a star member of the Metropolitan Opera audience. During my years as general manager I always knew when she was in the house. Her carefully staged entrances were entrancing; her measured acknowledgment of applause timed to perfection. When some soprano onstage was having problems with any of her great roles, especially the two Verdi Leonoras (*Il Trovatore* and *La Forza del Destino*), the curtain calls were often accompanied by murmurs and sighs of "Milanov . . . Milanov!" She captured the public with her artistry; she retained its affection by becoming a grande dame of opera.

I never think of her without recalling the splendid 1952 Thanksgiving celebration at my mother-in-law's country home in Plymouth, Massachusetts. That year our fellow houseguests included Edward Johnson, then just retired as Metropolitan general manager. Johnson had introduced Milanov to the American public in the late 1930s; by the 1950s she was in her prime, a prima donna *assoluta* in every sense of the phrase. And that didn't always make life easy for the general manager.

During predinner cocktails, Johnson, impeccably dressed, smilingly at ease, began telling stories about his "Yugoslav princess," how he and Artur Bodanzky had heard her special audition in Prague in June 1937 and wanted to bring her to the Met immediately, how hearing of her spectacular success in the Verdi *Requiem* at Salzburg under Toscanini just two months later had strengthened his resolve all the more. He described his courtship proceedings, the on-and-off conversation, her coyness, the flirting, batting of eyes, the almost agreements, the rejections. She was not at all happy with the seventy-five dollars a week he was offering. He spoke of being driven half-mad by this Rubenesque woman with the sharp peasant mind and the glorious voice.

At the time she was married to the actor Predag Milanov, who alternately encouraged and resisted Johnson's blandishments and finally proved irritating enough to the essentially genial general manager that he gave up. On his last night in Europe, however, an unexpected telephone call swept aside all his previous discussions and confirmed her acceptance of his "final" offer, $125 per week.

Her Met debut, in December 1937 in *Il Trovatore,* was not the sensation he hoped or she expected; she was ready to return immediately to Europe. He persuaded her to stay. Within a short time she had a huge success as Aïda; then she wanted to renegotiate her contract. "I love her," he said, smiling, "but now Mr. Bing will have to attend to her wants. All I have is the pleasure of her voice."

He did, of course, as did we all. Her last performance onstage was during the final night at the old opera house; her first night in the audience at the opening night of the new house at Lincoln Center in 1966. Until her death in 1989, the Met was, in a very real sense, her home. It is a sadder place without her.

ZINKA MILANOV

New York City
April 3, 1987

She resisted everything as I set up—lights, backdrop, makeup. "Perhaps, Madame Milanov, you will wear a gown or something 'regal'?" "Vhy? Clothes make the artist? No, I will not. I just use little leopard scarf." She sat and I began lighting her face. "I always had a byu-ti-ful smile," she said—clearly relishing the fuss, but still determined to play the grande dame!

—J.D.R.

Giulietta Simionato

I never had the privilege of working with the enchanting Giulietta Simionato; would that I had. Part of the reason is that she unexpectedly retired from the lyric theater in 1966, when her career was still in full flower, in order to become the wife of one of Italy's most celebrated physicians, Dr. Cesare Frugoni. Dr. Frugoni died in the 1980s at the age of ninety-seven; happily Signora Simionato-Frugoni is still very much with us.

Simionato's decision to marry the good doctor had apparently been made some time before they actually wed. She had made up her mind that once all the complications to the marriage (the most serious of which was at that time in Italy there was no divorce, and Frugoni's wife had been in a mental hospital for many years) were swept aside, she would marry him and quit the stage. When the first Signora Frugoni died and the way was cleared for them to marry, Giulietta retired quietly on February 1, 1966, the approximate anniversary of her debut at La Scala thirty years before as one of the Flower Maidens in *Parsifal.*

As Lanfranco Rasponi reported in *The Last Prima Donnas,* Simionato asked La Scala's artistic director at the time, Luigi Oldani, what opera was scheduled for the night of February 1. When told it was to be *La Clemenza di Tito* at the Piccola Scala, she insisted on having a part in it. "But all the roles have been assigned," he replied. "Never mind," she retorted. "I don't need an important part. I want to sing on that date for nostalgia's sake. Please do me this favor." Surprised at her request, he assigned her the role of Servilia for just that one performance; she learned it in a few days.

No one had been let in on the secret, but when the makeup artist came to her dressing room she asked him to do an especially good job because this was to be her last performance. The news spread quickly among the stage personnel, and then soon reached the public. No one could believe it, and the performance ended with the audience stomping and in tears.

Simionato began her career as a *comprimàrio* at La Scala in 1936. As she explained to Rasponi:

GIULIETTA SIMIONATO

Secaucus, New Jersey
September 20, 1989

Giulietta Simionato, Renata Tebaldi, and actress Valentina Cortese are good friends. (Cortese, incidentally, is Simionato's sister-in-law, their husbands the de Angeli brothers, the pharmaceutical magnates.) And so it is a familiar sight to see these three legends sharing a box on opening night at La Scala. All eyes are upon them, resplendent in their jewels and array. All three are beautiful: the Three Graces. Simionato was approaching eighty when she sat for these photographs, and she proves that beauty defies age.   —J.D.R.

I was handed a contract the likes of which I don't think ever existed. I had to be ready with every role, *comprimàrio* and otherwise. I was assigned, among other roles, to be the maid in the second act of *Manon* in a glittering production starring Gigli and Favero. All I had to do was bring in the coffee on a tray and utter a brief sentence. Well, I upset the pot and remained completely silent. I still got to sing a string of secondary roles but nothing positive was really moving.

Nothing much did happen until shortly after World War II, when she was approached one night by a former singer turned opera manager who was organizing several operatic seasons in Switzerland. The La Scala management granted her request for leave, and in Switzerland she sang her first Cherubino, her first Dorabella, and Fidalma in *Il Matrimonio Segreto.* The notices were superb, and the news of them traveled back to Italy where in April 1947 she was finally assigned Dorabella at La Scala. It was her first leading role in that great house. In Simionato's own words:

> From then on, every leading mezzo role was thrown at me, not only at La Scala, but all over Italy and abroad. Cinderella became a hard-working princess. . . . When I exploded at last, and quickly gained recognition, everything came my way. I became a regular member of the Vienna Staatsoper and appeared regularly at the Salzburg Festival. Along with the Metropolitan (where I only appeared in four roles, and then as Dalila on tour) I sang everywhere, including London, Mexico City, Tokyo, Chicago, Hamburg, Rio de Janeiro, and . . . the world.

My discovery of this extraordinary artist came on opening night of the Met's 1959–1960 season. For the first time in the company's history *Il Trovatore* was chosen for this musical/social occasion. Simionato made her Met debut in the role of Azucena, capturing the heart of the often erratic opening-night audience and going on to charm and delight New York with her rich, strong voice and her command of acting.

Those of us who saw and heard her in person would, I think, agree with the words of the late Gilda dalla Rizza: "There have been many great singers, but few will leave a permanent place for themselves in the history of opera. Of the group who came after me, I would put Simionato at the top of the list, not Callas. They talk about Callas singing everything; yes, but how? With three voices, and only the coloratura was, for a few years, impressive. But Simionato sang everything, and with only one wonderful voice. She became a luminous star not through publicity, but through exceptional merit."

Marilyn Horne

॰॰॰॰॰

Marilyn Horne—"Jackie" to her friends, a nickname given her by her older brother, Dick, because he wanted her to be a boy and had already picked the name before she was born—has one of the most remarkable voices of our time. Its texture is warm, powerful at the bottom and brilliant at the top, and her way of using it reminds one of a skier careering down slopes, making spectacular leaps and turns but always landing with absolute accuracy. Her range has permitted her to sing every kind of music and play every kind of operatic role, from the timid Mimi of *La Bohème* to the most exacting parts of the bel canto repertoire. She is also, hands down, the most exciting and sexy Carmen of our time, a role with which she'd had scratchy luck until she sang it at the Metropolitan Opera on September 19, 1972, and overnight became a prima donna *assoluta*.

Her Met *Carmen* saga started with Bing's named successor, Goeran Gentele, intendant of the Royal Opera in Stockholm. Gentele was to officially take office on July 1, 1972, but actually joined the company in the fall of 1971 for a year of observation. Earlier

that same year, after repeated meetings, I agreed to become his assistant general manager.

During the winter of 1971, Gentele flew in and out of New York from Stockholm for a number of preliminary meetings on repertoire. Because of the pattern of international opera life, Bing had largely planned what would be Gentele's first season, including an opening night *Tannhauser.* Gentele was willing to let this stand until he actually saw the production, a tattered mess of decaying costumes and decrepit scenery. Around the opera house it was referred to as "Bing's revenge." Gentele immediately set about remedying the situation, bearing in mind that his substitute opera had to suit his already-contracted stars: Marilyn Horne, James MacCracken, and Tom Krause.

He quickly settled on *Carmen,* not the usual watered-down *Carmen,* a hideous production of which was then in the Met's repertoire, but the original concept that premiered at the Opera-Comique in Paris on March 3, 1875. Spoken dialogue had been employed then; it was only after Bizet's death that musical recitatives were subsituted by the composer's friend, Ernest Guiraud, whose version was quickly adapted and used around the world.

MARILYN HORNE

*New York City
April 7, 1992*

As I photographed Horne, I asked her to think the music to a song her good friend Portia Nelson had written, "Make a Rainbow." She became lost in reverie, and a certain softness crossed her face. Nine months later, January 21, 1993, she touched the world as she sang that same song at the Presidential Inauguration of Bill Clinton.

—J.D.R.

When Gentele asked his board for the money to mount his new and original production—and they quickly agreed—he persuaded Leonard Bernstein to conduct and Josef Svoboda to design what he had in mind. The three principal singers were delighted, especially Marilyn Horne, who in her autobiography wrote that "If a mezzo said her prayers before she went to bed, they might end . . . 'and please, God, give me *Carmen* for opening night at the Met.'"

During the winter, spring, and early summer of 1972, Gentele spent a lot of time putting *Carmen* together. During preliminary sessions, the work was discussed and rediscussed, analyzed and reanalyzed, and when there were unresolved points, he kept telling everyone they'd be resolved in rehearsals. A former actor himself, he knew that artists and directors flourish in give-and-take situations.

But it was not to be. On July 18, 1972, while vacationing in Sardinia, Goeran Gentele was killed in an automobile accident, leaving the Met not only without a permanent general manager but also without a director for the opening *Carmen.* The Met board appointed me acting general manager and I, with Bernstein's approval, turned the production over to Bodo Igesz, Gentele's assistant director, who'd been at his side during most of the early conferences.

JAMES McCRACKEN

New York City
September 24, 1986

On stage he was an explosive force. Off stage he was without ego . . . rather sheepish, like the high school student embarrassed to give a speech in front of his class.

—J.D.R.

As Bernstein and Igesz began working together, there was considerable speculation among opera buffs as to what would finally happen on this bedeviled production. Everybody knew Jackie could toss off the vocal aspects of Carmen, but would she make a great Carmen as an actress? Would James McCracken, one of the most powerful of tenors, exhibit the lyricism, tenderness, and fury that the role of Don Jose demands? Would Bodo Igesz be able to modify the talents of all the artists involved in order that a beautiful whole would be achieved?

Jackie Horne and I were in frequent touch during those trying days because she was troubled about a number of aspects of the production, especially the dialogue. She thought English-speaking audiences would be uncomfortable without the Guiraud recitatives, and that the spoken French would be too much for them. She finally yielded on this point to Bernstein, but then she was upset by the starkness of the mise-en-scène, especially the fact that the stage was to be covered with a gray carpet. She insisted the carpet would absorb sound, and it was only after Bernstein asked McCracken to let fly that she accepted the fact that the carpet was made from nonabsorbent material. But on one point she threatened withdrawal: there was no prompter's box.

The prompter's box is usually a small compartment placed in between the foot-lights and covered on three sides. The prompter inside is visible only to the participants onstage; his job is to cue the singers by giving them the first words. In Europe, the prompter's box is de rigueur; La Scala even has two of them, one for the soloists and one for the chorus. But Gentele hated this custom; Jackie, however, made it clear that such an elimination would be a ticket to disaster. Since the person in the box literally holds the production together during a performance, she didn't intend to let that person be swept away by Svoboda's carpet. Her point was accepted; the box was restored.

She won another victory as well. The late James McCracken was, as she described him, a "pussycat," except when he came to a part, and then he literally became the character he was portraying. At the first rehearsal of the final scene of the opera, where Don Jose stabs Carmen as she tries to go past him into the bullfight arena, she heard a click and looked down to see a real switchblade in Jimmy's hand. "There's no way you're going to get me on that stage if Jimmy McCracken has a real knife!" she said loudly. Jimmy was properly chagrined—and disarmed.

McCracken's intensity also flared at the jam-packed *Carmen* dress rehearsal. In the second act, when Don Jose starts getting passionate, he was struggling to get his sword off. The scabbard wouldn't loosen, and he had to keep yanking and tugging as he declaimed *"Ah, que je t'aime, Carmen, que je t'aime!"* The situation was irresistible to Jackie, who in clear English answered his impassioned declaration with, "Sure, Jimmy, as soon as you take your sword off!" The audience collapsed with laughter.

On September 19, 1972, the miracle occurred. Jackie was a sensation, critics comparing her to the celebrated Bruna Castagna, a great Carmen of Edward Johnson's regime at the Met. McCracken proved to be a Don Jose of such vocal mastery that he sang the last note of the "Flower Song" pianissimo, a trick that few tenors in modern times have ever been able to bring off. But it was Jackie's night, and she relished every moment of it.

Before Gentele's death, the two of them had talked about bringing important fresh repertoire to the Met, especially for her, including a wide range of underheard Rossini operas. One of these, *L'Italiana in Algeri,* had been his first choice, and she enthusiastically accepted the production for the 1973–1974 season. I saw no reason to alter these arrangements.

L'Italiana in Algeri is an opera buffa about a shipwrecked young lady named Isabella, who is washed up on the Algerian shore where she immediately sings *"Cruda sorte"* ("Cruel Fate"), a bravura aria which has shipwrecked many a singer. Isabella is looking for Lindoro, her missing boyfriend. She's warm and loving, but, in Jackie's words, "a combination of Joan of Arc, Florence Nightingale, and Susan B. Anthony. She knows exactly what she wants and makes sure she gets it." What she wants is to find her man, but she doesn't know he's a slave of Mustafa, Bey of Algiers, who, tired of his wife, wants Lindoro to take her so that he can find an Italian girl for himself. Of such in-out-around-about plots are opera buffas made, and they're usually about as theatrically effective as yogurt. In this one, however, we benefited from Jean-Pierre Ponnelle's understanding of Jackie's comic strengths and taste. He designed, staged, and directed the production for her and created a truly funny entrance: she backed her way downstage and suddenly turned in wide-eyed astonishment to face the audience. The result was laughter and applause even before she opened her mouth.

Some critics, particularly the *Times*'s, grumbled about *L'Italiana,* praising Jackie's singing but calling the production "vulgar." The public, however, came in droves. We gave them an opportunity to hear this masterpiece for the first time in fifty years.

Since its November 1973 success, the Met has revived it three times, twice with Jackie. It's still in the repertoire, presumably waiting for an artist to come along with something approaching the Horne magic. *"Jedes Ding hat seine Zeit"* (Time, that thief, is passing). That's what Lotte Lehmann once told Jackie. Of course, it's true, yet somehow, because of common sense, the ability to judge her talent in a cool way, luck, and a strong constitution, she's managed to hold back the odds. She closes her autobiography with: "I must absorb everything while I'm still singing and step onto the stages of my many 'homes,' and look at the familiar surroundings, at the people who have come to hear me, to hear music. I must drink in everything because I want to remember everything . . . everything."

The Tenors and Bassos

Richard Tucker

Before joining the Metropolitan, I firmly believed that sopranos ruled opera. One always read that in the good old days Patti and Melba and their colleagues held opera houses in perpetual terror. Patti always insisted on being paid before the curtain went up: no money, no performance. Melba was a holy terror; she became, as Harold Schonberg describes in *The Glorious Ones,* the "archetype of the prima donna—rich, spoiled, outspoken, jealous of competition. She defended her territory and would not let anybody enter it without a royal fight." Stories of similar behavior and attitudes have been attached to sopranos throughout history, but it did not take me long to discover that sopranos pale when it comes to the real temperamentalists— the tenors.

There is nothing really new about this. As early as the 1850s, Max Maretzek, who produced and conducted opera in the United States, despaired of the species in his book *Crotchets and Quavers.* He described one Signore Lorenzo Salvi as someone who "believed himself in the Operatic world a fixed star, around whose twinkling luster . . . all the other planets had slowly and respectfully to revolve. . . . I felt he believed himself to be the Louis Quatorze of the lyric drama, and at times was under the impression that I should hear him exclaim: '*L'Opera, c'est moi!*'"

Signore Salvi was not alone. In 1852, Berlioz wrote in his book *Evenings with the Orchestra* about the musical sins of great tenors: "The tenor lords it over everyone and tramples on everything," he said. "He struts around the theater with the air of a conqueror; his crest gaily glints about his proud head; he is king, hero, demigod, god." Some decades later, George Bernard Shaw observed that "good tenors are so scarce that the world has always condoned any degree of imbecility for the sake of *ut de poitrine*—that is, a stentorian high C."

RICHARD TUCKER

From a bronze by sculptor Milton Hebald. —**J.D.R.**

During my time at the Met, it did not take me long to realize that all the comments—which may have been exaggerated and amusing to read about—turned out, in large measure, to be true. I spent an enormous part of my operatic life soothing, cajoling, and comforting the tenors while trying to understand their complicated psyches and praying they would honor their contracts. I had adventures with all of them, but a few stand out as especially memorable, not only because their names on the marquee generally meant hefty sellouts, but because they were—and two of them still are—superb artists.

Interestingly enough, Corelli, Domingo, and Pavarotti were all helped by, and drew inspiration from, Richard Tucker. He was the standard-bearer—"the master of us all" was the way Pavarotti put it. Certainly his discipline, breadth of repertoire, and professionalism served as an unmatched guide for his colleagues.

My own experiences with Tucker began in the 1950s, when I was part of his professional management team. From the day I met him until the last time we saw each other, about three weeks before his death, his physical presence hardly changed. He had the traditional tenor build: short and stout with a huge chest, thick arms and hands, and what must have been rope-sized vocal cords. In addition, he was bald and always wore a toupee, perhaps the best hairpiece I've ever seen on anyone. You had to look hard

to notice it and when you did you also saw that its color and texture blended perfectly with his remaining natural hair.

Tucker started life in a most unlikely setting for a future operatic superstar—the Williamsburg section of Brooklyn, New York—where he was born in 1913, the sixth and last child of Israel and Fannie Ticker. The Tickers were an immigrant Jewish family who, like thousands of others before them, had crossed the Atlantic in steerage, leaving behind the oppression of eastern Europe. Tucker's father, a farmhand and occasional peddler, came from Sucharan in the Carpathian Mountains near the Russian border of northern Rumania. He entered America with no skills whatever, and only the generosity of a Rumanian synagogue and a settlement house on the Lower East Side of Manhattan kept his family from starving. Israel Ticker quickly Americanized his first name to Sam, got a job in a candy store selling chocolate, and with the money he earned moved his family to the tenements of Brooklyn. There, on August 13, 1913, Fannie presented him with a baby boy. At the infant's *bris* he was named Rubin.

Rubin, or Ruby as he was soon called, brought a measure of luck with him at birth; Sam found a job in Manhattan's garment district, in the Jewish-dominated fur market. He had found his niche; the family was never again supported by charity.

Sam Ticker was an Orthodox Jew. He remained devout and observant despite his rigorous work schedule, but apart from the religious example he was a remote father. Fannie Ticker, on the other hand, was apparently warm, outgoing, and affectionate. A reasonably literate woman, she reinforced her children's identities as Jews, underscoring the meaning of the Book of Jonah: "I am a Hebrew, and I fear the Lord, the God of Heaven, Who hath made the sea and the dry land."

At the age of six, young Ruby Ticker was discovered to have a beautiful alto voice and was accepted as a choirboy by Cantor Samuel Weisser of the Tifereth Israel synagogue on the Lower East Side. Cantor Weisser was highly respected as a singer but especially as a teacher. In later years, Tucker would recall Weisser's tutelage, especially his apparent ability to make the youngster feel totally at home with the joy and pleasures, not the agony, of singing.

When Tucker and I first met, I was just beginning my career in the concert management business and knew little about his background other than the fact that he was a great tenor. I knew vaguely that he was a devoted Jew and strong family man and that his wife, Sara, was the sister of another remarkable tenor, Jan Peerce. I thought it rather extraordinary that two such brilliant voices were to be found in the same family. I quickly learned that the family tenors were never to be spoken about in the same breath. Both were stubborn and proud, and while no one incident seems to have driven them apart, they nonetheless detested each other. Peerce seems to have viewed Tucker as narcissistic, a man whose intelligence and social demeanor were distinctly below Peerce's own; Tucker saw Peerce as a spiteful man who hid petty hatred under the cloak of religion. "I don't go showing my dirty laundry in public," Tucker once said, "but when people ask the question 'How is it you two brothers-in-law don't get along?' I say it's simple. There's one word— jealousy. This man can't take it when anybody surpasses him."

Curiously, both men avoided criticizing each other in two areas, as family men and as tenors. Peerce, in his autobiography, called Tucker "a great tenor who had a great career." Tucker, in his oral history for the American Jewish Committee, said of Peerce: "To me he was always a great artist."

Ironically, it was their destiny to compete with each other at the Metropolitan, singing the same roles for the greater part of their professional lives—Tucker for thirty seasons and Peerce for twenty-seven. From my standpoint, there were also no difficulties; Peerce's professional affairs were in the hands of Sol Hurok, Tucker's in Arthur Judson's, the man for whom I worked.

Tucker, however, rarely used his concert agents to negotiate his arrangements with the Metropolitan Opera. He usually took care of those matters himself, having been brought directly to the company by Edward Johnson to make his debut there on January 25, 1945, as Enzo Grimaldo in Ponchielli's *La Gioconda.* He was, in a word, sensational. "With the stage to himself in the climax of the second act," said the *New York Herald Tribune,* "he seized the moment and won an ovation normally reserved for a Martinelli or a Melchior." Summarizing all the critics' judgments, Irving Kolodin put it this way:

"When Tucker finally decided to give his major effort to opera, the Metropolitan acquired its most beautiful tenor voice since Gigli."

For a while, comparisons to Gigli were mentioned in many critical reviews, the sign, perhaps, of a splendid beginning, but it was the words of his voice teacher and new Met colleague Paul Althouse that Tucker latched onto for life. Shortly after the reviews were published, Althouse turned to his young colleague and said: "I don't want you to sound like Gigli, Lauri-Volpe, Pertile, Paul Althouse, or anybody else. I just want you to be Richard Tucker—that's all, and that's enough."

And that's exactly what he did, from 1945 until his death in 1975, in synagogues, concert halls, recording studios, and especially opera houses the world over.

At the Met, he was always on time and fully prepared for rehearsals and performances. The actual day of a performance he would not speak; Sara became his interpreter. He would arrive at the theater precisely at 6:15 P.M. and walk briskly down the long corridor to his dressing room. His posture would be ramrod straight, his expression intense.

In his dressing room he would rest quietly, usually in a crimson robe, reviewing parts of the score of the evening. At 7:00 P.M. he moved to the large swivel chair in front of his dressing room mirror, where Victor Callegari, the Met's chief makeup artist, would begin to transform him into the character of the evening. At 7:30 P.M., still in his robe, he would break his silence and begin to sing, softly at first, then gradually louder. "I don't go in for long warm-ups," he often told people. "A pro is always ready." His warm-up routine lasted one minute and forty-five seconds. Hairstylist Nina Lawson and wardrobe chief John Casamassa would then dress him in costume and wig, and at 7:45 P.M., ready to go onstage, he would telephone the other dressing rooms to wish his colleagues good luck. If one of them was particularly nervous, he would comfort him or her with a hug or whisper something to the effect that together they were going to give the audience a hell of a show. Unlike many of his colleagues, he did not have competitive stage fever.

But when it came to business matters connected with his career, he was shrewd, determined, single-minded, and often slippery about moving and ducking around contract dates. He looked upon himself as the greatest tenor in the world and expected to be treated that way by every opera manager, concert impresario, or record producer with whom he came in contact; these feelings were with him right from the beginning of his career.

In 1949, for example, when he approached his first negotiations with Sir Rudolf Bing, he was warned that he would be dealing with a cold and calculating man.

"Listen," said Tucker to Thea Dispecker, then his personal advisor, "I don't give a damn whether he's cold as ice or hard as a brick. I'll wear him down and I know how to do it. You see, *I* know what I'm worth."

At that meeting Tucker insisted that his fee should be $750 a performance (remember, this was 1949); Bing offered him $450 a week. From 11:00 A.M. until after 1:00 P.M. the two men argued, Bing sitting straight on his chair, Tucker bouncing up and down and around the room. At one point he suggested they could settle everything over a nice lunch. Said Bing: "This is a business transaction, Mr. Tucker. I do not negotiate contracts at a lunch table. We will do business in this office, and only in this office. Lunch will have to wait until some other day."

Finally Bing issued what he called a last offer: $700 per performance.

"No," Tucker shot back. "Seven hundred and fifty! Not one penny less! We're haggling over fifty dollars; let's flip a coin for it."

"Let's do *what?*" Bing asked.

"You know, flip a coin," Tucker went on. "Let's say if it's heads, you win and I get seven hundred dollars. If it's tails, you pay me seven hundred and fifty. Fair enough?"

Before Bing could reply, Tucker took a quarter, handed it to Miss Dispecker, and told her to toss it into the air. Bing came around from behind his desk in time to see the coin land on his carpet.

"Heads! *Damn!*" Tucker exclaimed. "As the saying goes, Mr. Bing, 'Win some, lose some.' Today I had the luck of the Irish. The hell of it is, I'm Jewish. So seven hundred it is!"

Many years later Bing and Miss Dispecker were reminiscing. "Shall we say it was the most unorthodox negotiation I can recall?" was Bing's comment.

On the matter of repertoire, Tucker always felt he knew what his fans expected. During our days together at Columbia Artists and later when I was director of Masterworks at Columbia Records, his principal recording label, I tried to persuade him to look at some Schubert and Hugo Wolf with the idea of a liederabend.

"No, kid, that's not for me," he would say. "My fans wouldn't like it."

I tried to suggest that with his voice, and given that every important conductor always talked about his extraordinary musicianship, perhaps he should expand the interest of his public. He'd smile and shake his head.

"Sorry, kid, the fans want arias and full operas. And that's what I'm going to give them."

While to this day I still feel I was right, there was no arguing his feeling and judgments about his fans. I suspect he loved them as much as they loved him, and he certainly took their assorted comments to heart. A case in point was the Met's revival of Tchaikovsky's *Eugene Onegin* in the late 1950s. Tucker sang Lenski, supported by a strong cast including George London as Onegin, Rosalind Elias as Olga, and Lucine Amara as Tatiana. Tucker was uncomfort-

SIR RUDOLF BING

New York City
April 2, 1986

He once made a statement which reflected his singular life: "Managing a famous opera company," he said, "means being entrusted with the works it has taken three hundred years of genius to create. Working as Manager of the Metropolitan I have always tried to be faithful to that trust." Now he whiled away time sitting in the lobby of the Essex House or on a park bench, a lone figure aimlessly watching passersby. Being photographed meant sharing company with someone. "I hope I'll see you again," he said to me as I bid goodbye. "Come back anytime." —J.D.R.

able in the role and dropped it quickly from his repertoire. He later told the press: "My public doesn't like me in a role where I die in the second act."

Dying in the second act, or indeed acting at all, was never one of Tucker's strongest talents—at least not until he undertook the role of Canio in *I Pagliacci.* Curiously, he had recorded the opera in both 1949 and 1951 but did not appear onstage in the part until 1970, at the age of fifty-six. He was always extremely careful about choosing his opera house roles, waiting until he felt ready for the combination of physical stage action and singing. Perhaps as a result of this caution, Canio was his greatest single operatic achievement, both musically and dramatically, and for this much of the credit goes to the director, Franco Zeffirelli.

When the two men began working together, Zeffirelli's insights led him to see a private man, the "real" Richard Tucker, whose basic nature was not dissimilar to Canio's essential character: explosive energy contained only by hard-learned self-control. Tucker himself was, indeed, such a man, not possessed, as is Canio, by jealousy and basic insecurity, but fully capable of losing his strong temper if betrayed by people and circumstances. In this basic similarity, Zeffirelli found and shaped a Canio that no one who saw or heard is likely to forget.

Despite his white-hot success in this role, however, Bing denied Tucker the one production he yearned to have mounted for him, Jacques Halevy's *La Juive.* The libretto of *La Juive,* by Eugene Scribe, is basically the story of Christian-Jewish conflict personified by two men, the Catholic Cardinal Brogny and a wealthy Jewish goldsmith Eleazar.

Bing never understood that Tucker's obsession with this opera had little to do with the fact that Caruso sang Eleazar as his last role at the Met; it really had to do with the long and tragic history of life in the Jewish ghettos, particularly in the aftermath of the Holocaust. Tucker, a tolerant man, believed he had a part to play in unifying people, perhaps by showing, through Eleazar, that history's darkest ages must not repeat themselves.

Tucker began his quest for the role in 1962, reminding Bing that *La Juive* had been performed almost every other season at the Met from 1919 to 1935, when Caruso or Martinelli had sung Eleazar, but had not been mounted since 1935. He argued that he could sing Eleazar more definitively than any of his predecessors since he was, of course, a *hazzan.* Bing answered that no doubt he would be brilliant in the role but who would step in if he was indisposed? The matter rested there.

When I became general manager, one of our first conversations was about *La Juive.* I told Tucker that I thought he had a good idea but that we would have to wait for a couple of years until I sorted things out. He shrugged his shoulders and made it clear he was determined to perform this role anyplace that gave him an invitation.

"It's my part, kid," he said on more than one occasion, "and I've got somebody who'll pay for a Met production. I'll get Bernstein to conduct, and I'll line up the rest of the cast."

I reminded him that even though I was new on the job, I was aware that the general manager undertook those kinds of production responsibilities, but he never heard me.

"Just say the word and leave it to me, kid, leave it to me."

His obsession with this part soon led to a real crisis between us. During the 1973–1974 season he was to sing *Simon Boccanegra*, with Sherrill Milnes in the title role, and *Vespri Siciliani* with Renata Scotto as his leading lady. *Simon Boccanegra* had been absent from the Met repertoire for at least two seasons, and the combination of Milnes and Tucker in the two principal roles was strong box office; *Vespri Siciliani* was one of my first new productions and in these performances Tucker and Scotto were eagerly awaited by Verdi aficionados.

Some weeks before the first performance of *Simon Boccanegra*, Tucker came to my office asking to be released from his contract for the *Vespri* performances in order to accept an offer of *La Juive* in Barcelona. I told him I'd look at the schedule but doubted I could grant his request.

"Oh, come on, kid," he remonstrated. "There are lots of people who can replace me in *Vespri*."

"No there aren't, Richard, but I'll check other availabilities and let you know."

A few days later I called him to say that I was sorry but we'd have to stick to our contract. He was polite but matter-of-fact when I gave him the message, and I took the precaution of calling his agent to make certain he understood. I was assured he did.

Several weeks later, at the final performance of *Simon Boccanegra*, which happened to be the Saturday-matinee broadcast, Charles Riecker burst into my office with the news that Tucker was leaving for Spain that afternoon, walking out on his commitment for *Vespri*. I went down to his dressing room after the performance and confronted him.

"Is it true you're going to Spain?" I asked.

"Yeah, kid," he replied.

"But you have an agreement with us, remember? I couldn't release you because I wasn't able to find a replacement. You mean you're just walking out anyway?"

"That's right, kid," he answered, and then, coming over to me and placing a hand on my shoulder, he said: "Bill Lewis will be just great."

William Lewis was Tucker's cover, a splendid singer in his own right but not then a starring artist the public would pay to hear.

"Richard," I said, looking at him carefully. "You can't do this. You'll leave the Met in a mess."

"Ah, you'll be okay. Don't worry," he replied, patting me on the cheek, "I'll be back next season."

He left the dressing room and started down the corridor toward the stage door.

"Richard," I said, keeping pace with him, "if you do this there will be no Met for you next season. I mean it."

He stopped for a moment and looked at me.

"Oh, forget it, kid," he said, "you'll be just fine. You're doing a great job."

Before I could reply he was out of the stage door, signing autographs for the assembled fans.

I returned to my office and, calling together the artistic staff, gave them a full briefing.

"You know he pulled the same trick on Bing," exclaimed Riecker. "I remember it very well. He left the stage of the old house during a rehearsal, telling Bing he was off to Texas to sing *La Juive* and Bing called after him that if he left he needn't bother to come back. Of course, he didn't mean it, but he was mad as hell."

"Well, I do mean it," I said. "We've enough problems without putting up with this nonsense. I'm going to fire him."

And I did, on the following Monday. Over the next few days I found myself in a whirlwind. Trustees began calling, demanding to know what was going on. Mrs. August

Belmont, long retired from active participation in Met affairs, was on the telephone pleading his case. Critics were questioning my competence. I began receiving ugly mail from his fans, climaxed by a visit from a spokesperson for the regular standees, who informed me that not only had I made a bad decision but that I would soon regret the day I entered the Met.

As the weeks passed, however, I began to have second thoughts, not about the correctness of my original decision but about the facts of operatic life: I needed him. We were a big company performing a vast repertoire and there were simply not that many world-class tenors available. I consulted with my colleagues and they agreed we had to have him back, but we could not decide how to bring this about with tact and diplomacy and still make my point about contractual obligations.

While we were puzzling over the problem I received a call from his concert agent asking for an appointment. The agent, Michael Reis, was contrite and concise. Tucker wanted to return, what was the price? I told him the price was simple: I wanted a letter apologizing to the Metropolitan for his unwarranted behavior and a guarantee he would honor all his future contract obligations. Further, I wanted the letter to state that should he fail to do so I would, at the next defection, be free to hand his letter over to the media.

Reis accepted my idea, and later the same day Tucker called to discuss the following seasons. I told him such a discussion would wait until I had the letter I asked for firmly in my hands.

"You'll have it, kid, this afternoon," was his reply.

A messenger did, indeed, deliver a letter to me, but it was not what I wanted. I called Reis and dictated the correct text.

"No tricks, now," I added. "It's either my way or not at all."

"But think of his pride," Reis said.

"Think of the Met's," was my rejoinder.

The correct letter came the next day.

Tucker and I took up where we'd left off, as if nothing had happened. He told me of an upcoming *La Juive* he was singing in New Orleans and reminded me that he had a friend who would underwrite the production at the Met, if I wanted it. After a lengthy discussion I agreed to mount the work for him in the 1976–1977 season.

"You'll see, kid," he said, "you'll see! It'll be a great show."

Tucker returned to the roster early in the 1974–1975 season singing Canio, and what turned out to be his last performance at the Metropolitan, December 3, 1974, was almost prophetic.

That night, as part of a series of television experiments, we were taping both *Cavalleria Rusticana* and *Pagliacci.* My wife and I decided to go deep into the bowels of the theater to watch and listen on a television monitor. When Tucker made his entrance in *Pagliacci* he was absolutely electrifying—tortured, resentful, angry, passionate. There were several people clustered around watching with us, mostly television technicians, but it was only a matter of minutes before they, too, were as caught up in his performance as we were. By the time the opera ended, the control room crew were on their feet giving him an unseen ovation.

On our way up to the stage for the curtain calls, I remarked to Betty that he reminded me of a brilliant light, one of those powerful bulbs that has an extra burst of energy before it burns out. By the time we reached the stage the wild applause, punctuated by cheers and bravos and rhythmic clapping, could be clearly heard behind the closed curtain.

Tucker, in a totally uncharacteristic manner, was sitting on a corner of the set, pale and sweating with exhaustion. I went over to ask him if he was all right.

"I'm fine, kid, fine," he replied. "Just very tired. This is a tough piece, you know. Very tough."

At close range he looked haunted with weariness, like a combat soldier after days of skirmishes. He took a deep breath, got to his feet, and told the stage manager he was ready to take his curtain calls. He shuffled over to the curtain, grabbing hold of it with an iron grip, and then, straightening his shoulders, went out for his bows.

The roar from the audience was overpowering. He stood looking at them, absorbing energy from the tidal wave of their affection and approval. When he was finished we walked slowly back to his dressing room. Some color had returned to his face, but the old Tucker energy was at low ebb.

"Are you sure you're okay?" I asked.

"Yeah," he answered, "but don't say anything to Sara about my being tired. She's been after me to cut down, but I can't do that, kid. I'm great, just great. Don't worry."

I left him at his dressing room door but was troubled by my earlier thoughts of brilliant light before darkness.

The next day he called to say he was feeling fine and about to go out with his friend Robert Merrill for a brief joint concert tour.

"Piece of cake, the tour," he added. "Bob and I have a great time together. I'll see you in a few weeks and we'll settle everything about *La Juive.* It's going to be terrific!"

But it was not to happen; those were the last words we had together. About a month later, while on tour in Kalamazoo, Michigan, he collapsed and died from a massive heart attack. He was sixty-two years old.

On January 10, 1975, Tucker's funeral took place at the Metropolitan Opera House. Almost three thousand fans, colleagues, and friends filled the auditorium to pay their last respects, among them Franco Corelli, the only fellow artist whom Tucker ever envied. Their rivalry had, at first, been fierce. It began in 1960 when Bing assigned the young Italian to the role of Calaf in his new production of Puccini's *Turandot,* a role Tucker felt, by right and seniority, belonged to him. Corelli's success made Tucker feel that Bing now had a new favorite and it wasn't until some years later, when Corelli sought out Tucker for some professional advice, that their friendship began. The advice was simple: Corelli, having attended a rehearsal of *Tosca,* asked Tucker if he would sing *"O dolci mana."*

"I would like to see you sing it," Corelli asked, somewhat nervously.

Tucker was amused, and perhaps also a little touched by the request.

"To sing it right, Franco," he said, "you have to be Jewish!"

Corelli laughed.

Franco Corelli

With his striking good looks, athletic body, dark, brooding, and slightly panicky eyes, Franco Corelli was the only romantic tenor of his time who had the physical characteristics to match his voice. Sir Rudolf Bing once described him as "looking like a god."

All of his physical attributes aside, however, his voice was his greatest asset—powerful, colorful, clear, and ringing with just a hint of his original baritone. He had an almost animal energy that grabbed listeners and, for all intents and purposes, conquered them.

In spite of all these impressive qualities, however, Corelli's nervousness and deep insecurity were the undoing of his career. By the time I arrived at the Met he was famous for mysterious disappearances and last-minute cancellations. I hadn't been on the job for two days before I had my first run-in with these caprices: he failed to show up to rehearse Gounod's *Romeo et Juliette*. Bing had mounted the production of this seldom-performed work especially for him in the late 1960s; he knew the part and had sung it with great success, but for some inexplicable reason he wasn't in the theater when he was supposed to be. There were no letters, cables, or telephone calls, just silence. The Juliette, Anna Moffo, and the rest of the cast started rehearsals but were obviously handicapped by the missing Romeo. George Shirley, who was scheduled to cover and sing the role later in the season, agreed to fill in while we spread out an international net to locate our *primo tenore*. After many days searchers finally discovered him hiding in a small Italian mountain village where, for reasons unknown, he'd cut himself off from the outside world.

Corelli first entered my professional life in 1970, when, as Leonard Bernstein's producer, I engaged him to sing the Verdi *Requiem* in London for television taping, a recording, and an Albert Hall performance. We signed contracts for this triple project while the Met was on strike in 1969, and when that strike was settled, Bernstein, as a favor to his friend Franco Zeffirelli, agreed to conduct a few performances of *Cavalleria Rusticana* with Corelli singing Turiddu. The production was a new one, designed and directed by Zeffirelli, and Corelli seemed fine at the rehearsals, but minutes before the first performance, a Saturday-matinee radio broadcast, he appeared in Bernstein's dressing room looking wild-eyed and distraught. I noticed his costume doublet was buttoned all askew and his shirt was disheveled and sticking out in various directions.

"I can't sing this afternoon," he blurted out to Bernstein. "I'm too upset. I'll ruin the performance. I can't do it." He ran his hands through his hair while shaking his head.

Bernstein looked at him calmly during this outburst and at the right moment leapt to his feet.

"Corelli!" he barked, "listen to me! We have seven minutes before the broadcast begins. Go back to your dressing room, button your jacket properly, fix your shirt. You are Corelli, the great tenor. You'll be beautiful. Keep your eyes on me. *Merde, toi-toi, in bocca al lupo.*" And with that he walked him to the door and pushed him out.

I'd been sitting in the dressing room corner, watching and listening to this extraordinary moment and thinking about our upcoming London project. I said to Bernstein that I thought we ought to have a standby artist in case Corelli should back out, and we agreed I would try to engage young Placido Domingo as our safety net.

"Don't worry about this afternoon," Bernstein said as he walked toward the orchestra pit to begin the performance. "He'll be fine. Every tenor panics at the opening of this opera; some do it more dramatically than others. But do see about Domingo for the *Requiem.* We can't take any chances on that."

I reached Domingo who, in fact, had already been quite active replacing Corelli around the world and was reaching a point in his own career where he no longer wanted to

FRANCO CORELLI

New York City
February 28, 1986

Franco Corelli, Prince of Tenors rang through my ears as I fired away at each shot. This was the slogan that used to appear on flyers, posters, and programs. He had been my boyhood hero, making opera an event. Corelli—on my part—was the impetus in beginning this book. —J.D.R.

pick up tenorial pieces. We did agree, however, that if he was needed I would telephone from London at least three days before our performances.

It was just as well. When Corelli arrived in London, fresh from his triumphs in *Cavalleria Rusticana,* he sang a *Requiem* piano rehearsal with Bernstein that was a disaster. He bleated and bellowed and wandered all over the score. Bernstein was appalled; so was I. We decided to wait for one more rehearsal in case his problems had been brought about by jet lag or travel fatigue, but the next day, at the piano rehearsal with chorus and all the other soloists, he was even worse.

Bernstein, our television director Humphrey Burton, and I had a council of war. Corelli had to go; Domingo would be asked to fly over. I was to make the necessary financial settlement to buy up Corelli's contract.

That, as it turned out, became unnecessary. Very early the next morning Mrs. Corelli telephoned to say that Franco wasn't feeling well and they would leave later in the day for Milan. He canceled; we didn't owe him anything.

All this flooded back into my mind as I was facing the problem of *Romeo.* He never did show up at the opera house until after the first performance, and when he finally came to see me, he was very nervous. He told me he'd been ill and upset by Gentele's death, and recalling our London episode, he said that he'd been ill there, too, and had not wanted to

ruin his reputation with Bernstein, with whom he'd had the "wonderful experience of *Cavalleria.*" I made no comment since I wanted to start our new relationship on an even keel, but I couldn't help wondering whether he had other cancellations up his sleeve. I was very careful to express sympathy with his problems and state my hopes that he would continue to be generous to the Metropolitan. We shook hands.

One afternoon, a few days after our meeting, I was sitting at my desk and suddenly noticed the familiar figure of Sir Rudolf Bing staring at me from outside the ground-floor window of my office. I motioned to him to come in, which he did, and the only thing on his mind was the future of Corelli. Bing had evidently seen him within hours of our first official meeting and was concerned I would take precipitous action to prevent his return in future seasons. I assured him I wanted Corelli around as much as he did.

"You know," Bing said to me, "he is the *great* singer today and the only one I care about."

I said I would try to make sure he continued to be active with us and hoped Sir Rudolf might make that clear to Corelli in any future discussions they might have.

Corelli himself began coming to rehearsals for his second production of the season, *Aïda,* and asking for *Romeo* coaching, since he was still scheduled for the broadcast performance of this work later in the season. I kept my fingers crossed that he would actually sing Radames, as originally planned. He did, much to our collective relief and the audiences' wild enthusiasm. Watching him in that part made it clear why both Aïda and Amneris could fall passionately in love; Corelli really sounded and looked like the ultimate hero.

Not too long after his *Aïda* success, he asked to see me.

"I have an idea," he said, looking much more in control of himself than I'd yet seen. "I want to study a new role and sing it on the spring tour."

"What role is that?" I asked.

"Macduff in *Macbeth,*" he replied.

"Macduff?" I answered. "Are you serious?"

"Very much serious," came his reply. "I know Macduff is usually sung by a *tenóre comprimàrio,* and I know there is only one big aria, but it is a wonderful role for acting and ensemble singing and I would like to do it."

I looked carefully at him to see if he was pulling my leg; Corelli asking to sing this important but modest role? His expression was serious and his attitude rather like a large schoolboy pleading before the headmaster.

"We'd be honored," I remember saying, "but will you have time to learn it before the tour starts?"

"Oh, yes," was his reply. "I would like to study now."

I took a quick look at the advance schedule and saw the opera was to be prepared by the late Alberta Masiello, the incomparable coach.

"I'll call Masiello and tell her what you want. I'm certain she'll be delighted." She was, but like me she was also essentially skeptical.

Truth to tell, in the press of other business I soon forgot about this project and was therefore totally bewildered when, some months later in Atlanta, the Corellis attended *Macbeth* and sat next to us.

"Is my dress rehearsal," he said, as the lights in the auditorium dimmed.

I looked at him politely but didn't have the vaguest idea what he was talking about.

At the end of the first act I sought out Charles Riecker, the artistic administrator.

"I've just had the oddest conversation with Corelli," I said. "He's sitting next to me and tells me this is his dress rehearsal. What's he talking about?"

"He's right," Riecker replied. "It is his dress rehearsal. He's singing Macduff in Dallas next week."

"You mean he's really learned the part and is serious about it?" I asked.

"Yes," said Riecker. "But don't worry. If he cancels we have three covers."

"But isn't this awfully expensive?" I asked. "I mean, if he actually sings it will be an artistic coup but a costly one."

"Don't worry," Riecker replied. "These performances won't cost us a cent. They're ones he owes us under his contract."

I thought of the missing Romeos and various cancellations and let it go at that.

The following week in Dallas, our opening performance was *Macbeth* and there, listed in the house program, was Corelli's name. Sherrill Milnes was the Macbeth; Grace Bumbry, the Lady Macbeth; and now Franco Corelli as Macduff. Pretty heady stuff. Heady enough so that when the late Lawrence Kelley, then impresario of the Dallas Opera, walked into the theater, he made a point of coming over to me and asking, somewhat condescendingly, where I was going to stand when making the announcement about Corelli's cancellation. I smiled, but none too securely. I had not yet gone backstage to wish everyone well, and felt certain that when I did I would find another body occupying the tenor's dressing room.

But I was mistaken; Corelli was right there. When I walked in he was having his wig and makeup adjusted. He looked almost serene.

"You will be here tonight?" he asked, turning away from his dressing room mirror to look right at me.

"Oh, yes," I answered. "I wouldn't want to miss this special occasion."

"Good!" he exclaimed. "I sing very well for you."

I went to my seat, whispering to Betty that he actually was going to perform. Lawrence Kelley was sitting alongside his principal supporter, a gorgonlike woman who reminded me of Oscar Wilde's comment from *The Picture of Dorian Gray:* "She has the remains of a truly remarkable ugliness." They both looked patronizing. I waved over to them.

That night the opera lovers of Dallas had the surprise of their lives. There, onstage, were three major artists feeding on each other's excellence. Corelli was superb, both vocally and as an actor. When he appeared to announce Duncan's murder, his distress and horror were palpable; by the close of the first act, all that glorious music was being sung by three balanced, powerful voices. When the curtain came down, the theater erupted.

Kelley and his friend accosted me during the intermission, this time with strikingly different attitudes.

"How did you ever persuade Corelli to take on this role?" Larry asked, with something approaching awe in his voice.

"Oh, just thought it might be a good idea," I replied, trying to look mysterious and all-knowing. "Splendid, isn't he?"

Backstage after the performance, Corelli was surrounded by his colleagues, all shaking his hands and hugging him, but when he saw us he broke away and came right over. After a polite bow and a "Hello, Signora Chapin," he turned to me and asked: "Did you like?"

I told him I liked a lot and was proud for him and the Metropolitan. He grasped my hand in both of his. For the remainder of the tour he sang every Macduff and audiences were thrilled.

In those days, when the national tour was over, we played an extra week of non-subscription performances back in New York. *Macbeth* was scheduled and I suggested to Riecker that Corelli ought to sing Macduff at home. But here we ran up against economic reality: all our "free" performances were gone. Unless I could persuade him to reduce his normal fee for what was essentially a supporting role, my managerial common sense had to come to the fore.

I broached the subject to him. His reaction was, to put it charitably, negative. I couldn't really blame him; he was one of the highest-paid singers on the roster and extremely shrewd about his position. I'm only sorry New Yorkers never got to hear him in one of his great artistic triumphs.

Triumphs, alas, were not always the order of Corelli's days. There were instances of horror, and one of these was an incident that demonstrated the sometimes incendiary nature of art and politics, particularly when two quick-tempered Italians are involved. I wrote briefly about this in my essay on Dorothy Kirsten, but saved the details for this particular chapter.

The conductor Carlo Felice Cillario was engaged for *Tosca*, one of the few operas that Corelli rarely canceled. Cavaradossi was a sympathetic role for him; he sang it with bravura and passion. On the occasion in question, Dorothy Kirsten was the Tosca, having flown in from California to pinch-hit for an ailing colleague. The performance was a non-subscription Saturday night and was sold out.

I should have known something was wrong when I went to see Corelli before the performance. He was sitting at his dressing table, staring into the mirror, brooding. As soon as I walked in, he quickly jumped up.

"Maestro Cillario. He doesn't like me," he said sharply. "We disagree about everything—tempi, politics, the world. I don't want to sing with him."

"Well," I answered, "perhaps you won't have to. The maestro will not be returning next season."

"Ah," he sighed nervously. "But we still have tonight."

"I'm sure everything will be fine," I answered. "After all, you're both professionals. *Toi-toi* for a good evening."

I went off to my box, settling in for one of my favorite operas. We'd asked several old friends to be with us and were looking forward to a good evening.

I should have known better.

The three crashing chords—the ominous motive of Scarpia—began the opera well, filled with tension and excitement. As the curtain rose the political fugitive Angelotti scurried around the stage, finally taking refuge in the Attavanti Chapel. The scene with the sacristan was amusing and presently Cavaradossi made his entrance. Corelli walked briskly onstage to enormous applause. Picking up his easel, he mounted the steps toward the portrait, adjusted his smock, and taking up the locket with Tosca's picture, began the beautiful aria *"Recondita armonia,"* which finishes with the impassioned line: *"Tosca sei tu!"* There were roars of approval and shouts of "Bravo Corelli!"

Now, there is a long-standing tradition that at this point in *Tosca* the conductor waits for the applause to die down before continuing. The tenor usually stays frozen in front of his easel, holding the locket, and allowing the audience's praise to wash over him. But on this night, Cillario didn't pause; over all the applause he continued to conduct. I saw Corelli turn and stare into the orchestra pit, his face a mask of fury. When he came to his next line: *"Fa il tuo piacere!"* he was almost yelling.

In the second act, Cavaradossi, having been brought to Scarpia and tortured to reveal Angelotti's hiding place, is dragged up from Scarpia's dungeons just as the news is brought of Napoleon's victory at Marengo. Cavaradossi confronts Scarpia by singing *"Vittoria! Vittoria! L'alba vindice appar . . ."* the *"Vittoria! Vittoria!"* being the only time in the act when the tenor has a chance to spin out two long solo notes. Corelli seized the opportunity to revenge himself for the first act; he held the notes longer and louder than I'd ever heard before, thus preventing the conductor from proceeding with the aria. When he finally dropped the first two words and continued, Cillario countered by increasing his tempo. But Corelli kept up with him. Further pandemonium was avoided, however, thanks largely to the libretto calling for Cavaradossi to be dragged offstage by Scarpia's police. By the time Dorothy Kirsten was ready to begin *"Vissi d'arte, vissi d'amore,"* some semblance of operatic order had returned.

Act III takes place on the roof of the Castel Sant'Angelo where Cavaradossi, having bribed his jailor, is writing his final love letter to Tosca. *"E lucevan le stelle,"* he sings. *"Oh, dolci baci, o languide carezze . . ."* The aria is the tenor's last big vocal opportunity. As it ends he bursts out sobbing and, covering his face with his hands, often sinks to his knees in despair. As with Act I's *"Recondita armonia,"* here again is a moment when the audience erupts into paroxysms of pleasure. Corelli had been at his best; the cheers and clapping were overwhelming.

This is also the other moment when the conductor traditionally pauses for the applause—but not on this occasion. Cillario pressed on. To my horror, and to the consternation of the audience, Corelli, an apoplectic look on his face, slowly stood up and stared into the orchestra pit, flipping his thumb between his teeth in the classic gesture of defiance, and walked off the stage. The audience began to groan "Oh, no!" Neighbors started talking to neighbors, boos could be heard in the distance; the smell of the mob was in the air.

Meanwhile, through all this hubbub, the orchestra continued to play, reaching the end of the ascending scale that signals Tosca's entrance. Tosca rushed onto the roof where she was first greeted by audience confusion, then no Cavaradossi, and a third problem: she was unable to start singing because she couldn't pick up her cue note. The orchestra's sound was overwhelmed by audience hysteria.

At the first sign of trouble I bolted from my seat and rushed backstage. There what can only be described as the "War for Tenor Independence" was in full cry. Corelli was screaming Italian epithets at Charles Riecker, gesticulating wildly, his eyes bulging and his fists clenched. I rushed between them and literally pushed Corelli back on to the stage.

There, Kirsten had finally found some kind of pitch and was singing her heart out to the spot where Cavaradossi would normally have been standing. When Corelli actually reappeared, she grabbed him firmly by both arms and forced him to look at her. Somehow her professionalism carried the day. As soon as the audience saw them together, the ruckus died down.

I stayed backstage for the remainder of the act. As Cavaradossi began walking up the steps to face the firing squad, one property man murmured that under the circumstances he was sorry he had not put real bullets in the rifles. When the shots rang out, a smattering of applause could plainly be heard among the backstage personnel.

Dorothy Kirsten finished the opera in grand style. I couldn't help thinking she must be greatly relieved at finally being able to leap over the parapet and bring an end to this particular performance.

As the house curtain came down, all hell broke loose. Corelli was on his feet, rushing down to the stage level with a mouthful of fiery words. When Cillario appeared from the orchestra pit Corelli leapt at him, getting his hands firmly around the conductor's throat. I tried to separate the two by forcing myself between them, but each was so intent on killing the other that I was squashed like soft sandwich filling. Riecker and three large stagehands came to my rescue, grabbing both combatants and separating them by holding their arms tightly to their respective sides.

Meanwhile, the audience was applauding and booing in about equal measure. Dorothy Kirsten went out for a bow and they cheered her enthusiastically. I turned to Corelli; to catch his attention I bellowed his name and told him to take a curtain call.

"Yes, Signore Chapin!" he said. Much to my surprise he walked out into the spotlight.

He was given an ovation, complete with torn-up programs as confetti. His public was entirely with him. I suggested to Cillario that perhaps this was not the night for a solo conductor bow. He agreed.

Finally, at the last curtain call of the night, Kirsten and Corelli came out together. Clasping her right hand he raised both their arms in a gesture of solidarity and victory. When they stepped backstage I ordered the iron curtain closed.

Franco Corelli gave each opera manager a whole assortment of problems, but in large measure he was worth the effort. When he was onstage, he looked and sounded heroic; getting him there, and keeping him content during a performance, was often a full-time challenge. His idiosyncrasies were legion.

For example, one of his biggest fears was a dry mouth. To combat this problem he hid wet sponges around the stage, tucking them into odd corners of scenery and into the bulges and folds of his costumes. During a performance, what might appear to be dramatic concentration was often masking a damp dab to the lips.

He often came offstage after a big aria, ringing his hands, convinced he was a disaster. On one such occasion, during a performance of *Turandot,* he sent for me in the middle of the first act.

"I sing so bad tonight," he said. "I no want to finish the opera. Please get my cover."

I told him his cover had left the theater and that if he quit now I would have to cancel the rest of the performance and refund the customers' money.

"Please, Franco," I said. "Don't make me do that."

He thought a moment and said: "I try, but you go out and tell the people I'm sick."

I did as he asked, just before the beginning of the second act. He finished the evening in glorious style, no longer nervous, I suspect, because his excuses had already been made.

The irony of these insecurities is that he had one of the greatest singing techniques of our time; there was almost nothing he couldn't do with his voice. His wife, Loretta, who almost never took her eyes off him in the theater or out, was a singing teacher and may have been the commanding force that kept him in first-class vocal condition.

His real problem was stage fright. Every appearance was a personal battle of nerves, and many times the nerves won. When he was younger he tried overcoming his difficulties by sticking to roles which vocally and dramatically were comfortable for him. As he grew older, though, the nervousness became a torture and the torture was finally too much to bear. It cost him his career.

I also discovered that underneath the insecurities, he was a cultivated man with a wide knowledge of and love for all the arts. Once, when we were in Detroit on tour, he took me through the European wing of the Detroit Art Museum, pointing out favorite pictures and talking about them with the ease and assurance of an experienced art historian. His calmness and security here were an abrupt contrast to his general state when facing his own profession.

Corelli's last performances with the Met were during the 1975 company tour of Japan. Here he sang another role that he almost enjoyed, Rodolfo in *La Bohème*. He was in good form, responding easily to the warmth of Japanese audiences and never canceling a performance. Part of the reason may have been that he and Pavarotti were alternating in the role; probably he didn't want his fellow countryman stealing the spotlight. Whatever the cause, his last days with the Metropolitan seemed curiously peaceful and unthreatened.

On the flight back from this particular trip, my wife celebrated her fiftieth birthday somewhere between Osaka and the international date line. As we were boarding the plane, Corelli sought her out and quietly presented her with a lovely bouquet of white orchids.

"I wish you all happiness, Signora Chapin," he said.

I thought to myself, as I heard him talking, that I really wished him exactly the same.

Jon Vickers

I met the Canadian tenor Jon Vickers for the first time in the fall of 1972, when he was in a smoldering rage over Sir Rudolf Bing's last artistic decision for the Met—to stage the 1971 Franco Zeffirelli production of *Otello*. This was the production in which, during the early months of my administration, he was to sing the title role for the first time in New York.

I'd been warned by our artistic administrator that Vickers hated everything about the production—the sets, costumes, and stage direction—and was threatening to withdraw from the cast. Knowing these facts, and with my heart in my mouth, I entered the theater during the first rehearsals to find Vickers standing in the center aisle, arms akimbo, staring at the stage. "What is this rubbish?" he hissed, pointing to the stern of Otello's ship. "Whose idea is it that the vessel sails into the harbor backward in the middle of a howling gale? It makes no sense. And those costumes with the fancy sleeves. Who'd wear a thing like that outdoors on a stormy night? Terrible, I tell you, terrible!" He glared at me. I suggested we discuss the matter outside rather than disrupt the stage crew. He walked slowly up the aisle shaking his head, and when we finally reached the outer lobby, he exploded.

It was my first experience with the Vickers temper. As expected, the verbal fireworks were gaudy but not the usual invectives one would expect; rather, a fierce sermon from a strong, disappointed minister addressing me as a careless member of his congregation. As he went along (and a lot of what he had to say made sense), he started pacing up and down, using his arms and hands to underscore his comments. At one point, out of the corner of my eye, I saw a colleague enter the lobby and smilingly approach the two of us. When he came within earshot he did the neatest 180-degree turn I've ever seen and dashed for the nearest exit.

Jon Vickers himself is a fascinating study in contradictions—a very private person who was, for a long time, in a very public profession. Like all great singers, he earned admiration as well as hostility. During his active career few were willing to detract from his voice, but he was often accused of being arrogant, aloof, and extremely difficult.

As critic John Ardoin once pointed out, however, much of this criticism grew out of the enormous contrasts within the man himself. Vickers shunned parties, interviews, and nonprofessional contacts with his colleagues. And yet, while he refused to engage a publicist, answer his critics, or indulge in self-serving ego trips, he often displayed a pressing need to be accepted and appreciated. One minute he could be the complete extrovert, clapping people on the back or sweeping them up and swinging them in the air; the next an introvert, returning a greeting with a blank look or with measured distance in his voice and manner. While he was fervently sought by all the major opera houses, he rarely made inroads with the stage-door fans.

Jon Vickers was catapulted into prominence in 1957 at the age of thirty, when Covent Garden mounted a landmark production of Berlioz's epic *Les Troyens.* Sixteen years later, during my second season as the Met's general manager, we finally brought that great opera to the Met stage with Vickers. In a very real sense, his career came full circle with *Les Troyens,* for that opera launched him internationally; when he repeated it in New York at the very height of his fame, he was the leading dramatic tenor of the day.

But in early November 1972, when he sounded off on his displeasure with the *Otello* production, *Les Troyens* was a year in the future. I didn't know whether he was going to honor any of his 1972–1973 commitments, including his incomparable *Peter Grimes,* or simply walk away from the Met never to return. At the end of our lobby shout, I would have bet on the latter. But then I just barely knew Jon Vickers.

A day after the tirade, Vickers arrived in my office accompanied by the young house director, Fabrizio Melano, whose job it was to restage the opera according to Zeffirelli's original stage plan. They sat down together while Jon explained his ideas to moderate some of what he perceived to be excessive stage business. Melano, a serious and independent young man, surprised me by his agreement with a great deal of what Vickers had to say. He also came up with some thoughts of his own. Both men were obviously on the same wavelength; I made it clear that as far as I was concerned, if they were in agreement the changes should be made.

But we were not yet out of the *Otello* woods. Five days before the dress rehearsal, the great Tito Gobbi, who was singing Iago, became ill and was forced to return to Italy. This left very little time to find a world-class substitute. Vickers was demanding to know with whom he would be singing; I kept putting him off while the artistic administration

JON VICKERS

New York City
April 15, 1987

Vickers is of a rare breed that demands a special title—a title all too often bestowed on others less deserving—that of singing *actor:* so totally is he able to immerse himself in a character and submerge his own personality. I deliberately set out to photograph Vickers not in costume, but nevertheless *assuming* the role of Peter Grimes. His Grimes could often instill terror: I lit his face accordingly, and Vickers, solely through his power of concentration, took on the countenance of the mysterious and feared fisherman. Studying the effects of light on his face, I became aware that Vickers was studying me. He broke the silence saying, "You work well, Jim." I was flattered yet sincerely touched, and he continued with words that, to this day, I hold as a maxim. He said, "Always remember: Those who touch the arts—be it the visual arts or the performing arts—must never lose sight of the original idealism that started them on a career. A person's talent must serve art; art must never serve the person. When you begin using the art form for your own glorification, it's time to get out."　—J.D.R.

combed the operatic woods. Finally we lucked out with another Canadian, the French Canadian baritone Louis Quilico, who was finishing up a West Coast engagement with the New York City Opera.

My sense of relief was short-lived; Vickers stormed into my office, asking if it was true that Quilico was replacing Gobbi. I told him it was. There then ensued a tirade about Canada. I was lectured about the differences between the philosophies of French and English Canadians and told sharply that I had no right to add to his considerable artistic burdens by placing him in the awkward position of having to work with someone he opposed politically.

By this time I'd really had enough. "You know, Jon," I said, looking him right in the eye, "why don't you save your anger for the performances? We're lucky to have Quilico, and if you have these feelings they might make great dramatic tension on the stage." He looked at me without comment and left the room, closing the door firmly behind him.

Quilico arrived and after his first rehearsals came to see me. He expressed surprise at Vickers's intensity about the production but made no mention of any conflict. I certainly didn't ask him!

On December 5, the tension-ridden *Otello* had its first performance of the season and Vickers sang one of the great interpretations of his career. Teresa Zylis-Gara was the Desdemona, matching him perfectly; the great duet at the end of Act I, *"Gia nella notte densa,"* melted one's heart. Quilico was a more than adequate Iago, although acting was not his strongest point. He did make it up with superior vocalism and the total effect was strong and dramatic. By the end of the opera I knew we were home free. During the curtain calls, Vickers's tension eased for the first time since I'd met him, helped by the public, who tore up programs and showered them down on him as an extra measure of thanks.

The next day he came to see me; the smiles were all gone. He'd been originally scheduled to sing four operas that season, *Otello, Die Walküre, Peter Grimes,* and *Pique Dame.* *Pique Dame* was just beginning rehearsals. "I've too much to do," he said, "too much, too many problems. I'm dropping *Pique Dame.* I just can't do it this year." By now I was beginning to know when to argue and when not. "I'm sorry, Jon," I replied. "We'll all be disappointed, especially the public, but I understand and will try to make other arrangements." He looked at me mysteriously, as if he hadn't expected my reaction to be quite so serene. "I'm so happy for all of us about *Walküre* and *Otello*," I went on, "and we all look forward to next season's *Les Troyens,* a reprise of *Otello* and *Tristan und Isolde.* I want you to be happy here, and we'll do anything we reasonably can to make you so." He sat back for a moment and looked sharply at me. My expression did not change.

"Well, we'll see about all that," he said after a few moments. "And in the meantime, no *Pique Dame.*"

In a real sense I breathed a sigh of relief. *Otello, Peter Grimes* and *Die Walküre* were still in place; I knew we had Nicholai Gedda for the first three *Pique Dame* performances, and William Lewis, an excellent cover, could take on Vickers's commitment. I felt we'd come through the 1972–1973 season with a working relationship and looked forward to further collaboration.

The 1973–1974 season began for Vickers on October 22, 1973, with a triumphant *Les Troyens.* He liked the Met's physical production and was comfortable with Nathaniel Merrill's stage direction and enormously supportive of Shirley Verrett who, because of Christa Ludwig's sudden illness, sang both Christa's part, Dido, and her own role, Cassandra, on the opening night. For the fall season he confined himself to singing Aeneas until January, when he was to take up *Tristan und Isolde,* first with Catarina Ligendza and then with the ultimate Isolde of our time, Birgit Nilsson.

I've already written in the Nilsson chapter of this book about what came to be known as the *"Tristan* crisis," when Ligendza, at literally the very last minute, canceled her contract, causing us to chase all over the world to find another Isolde for the three performances she was supposed to sing before Nilsson's arrival. Vickers's behavior during our search was far from helpful. When the American soprano Klara Barlow came to our rescue, he refused to sing the premiere with her, returning only for the radio broadcast performance as a warm-up. Then the magic all-can-be-forgiven night—when he and Nilsson sang the opera together for the first, and as it turned out only, time in New York.

That season he also returned to *Otello.* The first performance of *Otello* was to be broadcast. Teresa Stratas was scheduled to sing Desdemona, but at 11:00 A.M. on the broadcast Saturday, she called to cancel. Fortunately for all of us, Stratas was sharing the Desdemonas with a newcomer to the Met that year, the New Zealand soprano Kiri Te Kanawa. Te Kanawa was scheduled to make her formal debut several days later in the third performance of *Otello* and had actually rehearsed extensively with both Vickers and Thomas Stewart, the new Iago. I called her to explain it would be necessary to advance her debut to the premiere broadcast. She treated this information matter-of-factly, saying she'd come right to the theater for costume adjustments. I then took a deep breath and called Vickers. To my pleasant surprise, while concerned about Stratas, he assured me we had a winner with Te Kanawa and that he'd do everything possible to help her through the performance.

Those in the theater that afternoon, or who heard the nationwide broadcast, are not likely to forget the sensation of Te Kanawa's Metropolitan debut. After the final curtain, when the two artists came forward to take their curtain calls, Vickers took Te Kanawa by the hand and brought her to the front of the stage. Then, stepping back, he began applauding her himself as he moved out of the spotlight to let her be received by the audience alone. It was a gracious gesture of welcome to a new colleague.

My last professional association with Jon Vickers took place in the 1974–1975 season. Birgit Nilsson, in a surprise request, asked if we could rearrange Ring schedules to allow her to sing Sieglinda to Vickers's Siegmund in two performances of *Die Walküre.* Paul Jaretski, the resident Met genius on Ring matters, figured a way this could be done, and at the first performance with the two of them together in this intense opera, everything was going wonderfully until Vickers pulled the sword from the tree. He did this with such enthusiasm that the blade parted company from the handle and whistled past Nilsson's head en route to the safety net spread over the orchestra pit. Horrified, I rushed backstage to find Jon apologizing for his zeal while Nilsson, trembling, said that if she hadn't stepped back a step she would have lost part of her nose. The second performance was more dramatically cautious.

During all the experiences I had with this great tenor, I was struck over and over again by his dedication to artistic principles. He wanted the best, not only from himself, but from everyone connected with any of his projects. While he could be overpowering and extremely difficult, I have at the same time to say he was usually difficult for the right reasons. That didn't take away the need for the aspirin bottle; it just meant the pills were worth it.

The last time I saw and heard Vickers onstage he was singing the title role in a production of Berlioz's *Benvenuto Cellini* for Sarah Caldwell's Opera Company of Boston. In the cast, as the leading mime, was my oldest son, Henry Chapin, who was then a regular nonsinging member of Ms. Caldwell's company. My wife and I watched with fascination as the two played several scenes together.

After the performance we went back to pay our respects. Henry and Jon both greeted us warmly, but after Henry left what seemed like the male communal dressing room, Jon made it clear he appreciated our son's talent and dedication to his craft. "He and I feel the same way about doing things right," he said.

And as far as I was concerned, that was the ultimate accolade to Jon Vickers himself. He never stopped trying to do things the right way.

Giuseppe Di Stefano

W hat you see here is a photograph of a tenor whose voice and musicianship continue to be a major inspiration to colleagues everywhere, but whose own career was short-circuited by faulty advice and stubborn Sicilian-Milanese pride. Nevertheless, ask Carreras or Domingo or Pavarotti and they will tell you that Di Stefano's voice touches their souls. As Carreras put it in a recent interview: "To listen to Di Stefano is to be enveloped in emotions pouring out with the voice through the music."

His career at the Metropolitan began in 1948 with a thrilling Duke in *Rigoletto* and ended in the midfifties, when he and Sir Rudolf clashed over contracts.

Fortunately for all opera lovers, however, a collaboration with Maria Callas began in Mexico City during the late 1940s, when they performed together in *I Puritani,* and went on to include *La Traviata, Lucia di Lammermoor, Rigoletto* and *Tosca.* Triumph followed triumph, and in short order they became one of the greatest operatic duos of our time. In the 1950s their La Scala recordings began, right at the apex of their careers and in the full

GIUSEPPE DI STEFANO

Santa Maria Hoé, Italy
January 31, 1992
February 1, 1992

***Ultimi dei grande* (last of the great ones) . . . Di Stefano is the tenor's tenor. We spent a leisurely day photographing. The afternoon wound down, and Di Stefano, his young wife Monica, and I sat outside on the terrace drinking espresso. The sun was that four o'clock Italian sun—magic time— and as Di Stefano sat admiring the vista—the *colle Brianza* (hills of Brianza)—I grabbed my camera and captured one last image of Pippo.   —J.D.R.**

swell of their operatic achievements in Europe, South America, and the United States. Using the resources of that renowned opera house, they recorded the full range of their repertoire.

Their recordings became the criteria by which later versions by other artists were judged. *Tosca* was hailed by the *Washington Post* as "the most impassioned *Tosca* on records." *Newsweek* said it was "one of the finest operatic recordings ever to appear in the United States." Their vibrant vocal drama, their unique musicianship and charisma are to be found in *Il Trovatore, Manon Lescaut, I Puritani, Un Ballo in Maschera, La Bohème,* and many other works. Thankfully, Di Stefano and Callas recorded prolifically. Posterity will never be cheated of hearing a repertoire of truly inspired singing.

I'm always moved by Sir Rudolf's comments about the young Giuseppe Di Stefano:

"One of the most erratic artists with whom I had to work at the Metropolitan Opera was also one of the most gloriously talented. . . . The most spectacular single moment of my observation year had come when I heard his diminuendo on the high C in 'Salut! demure' in Faust. I shall never as long as I live forget the beauty of that sound."

Luciano Pavarotti

I met Luciano Pavarotti for the first time in September 1972 under melodramatic circumstances. At the end of the first week of my first season at the Metropolitan, I found I was dealing with what opera managers the world over have as their daily routine: artistic cancellations. In my case the first was Mirella Freni, bowing out of her contract for *La Bohème* because of what her cable referred to as "*your* Internal Revenue Service." Then came Tito Gobbi, stepping down from *Otello* because of illness, leaving us without an Iago. Then the conductor Erich Leinsdorf appeared in my office to demand another Wotan (he was rehearsing *Die Walküre*). All this took place within twenty minutes of my first seasonal Saturday morning, causing me, at one point, to close my office door, walk over to the window, and ask myself out loud: "You *wanted* this job?"

Those problems were all solved by the dexterity, commitment, and experience of the artistic administrative staff, but within a few days we fetched up with what really seemed to be the bottom.

On the morning of the *Otello* dress rehearsal my secretary appeared in the theater with the news that the scheduled evening premiere of *La Bohème* was in trouble. Freni had been replaced by Renata Scotto, but the problem was not the soprano; it was the tenor. Nicolai Gedda, usually the most reliable of all, was down with the flu. I asked who we had to replace him.

"No one," came the reply. "You're going to have to change the opera."

Now, changing the opera means refunding the audience's money, the very last thing any impresario wants to do. Somebody handed me a newspaper and pointed to a gossip column mentioning that Luciano Pavarotti had arrived in New York en route to Chicago for his season with the Chicago Lyric Opera. In those days Pavarotti was a major opera star but not yet a world celebrity. Among opera buffs, however, he was already a favorite. His ravishingly beautiful sound and his outgoing personality had begun to capture the public's imagination. He was not due at the Metropolitan until later in the season, but grasping at any possibility I called his hotel, introduced myself (we had never met), and asked if he would be kind enough to sing Rodolfo for us that night.

"Poor Gedda," he commiserated. "A shame for him." Then he paused a moment and took a deep breath.

"Okay, Mr. Chapeen," he said, "I do this for you. But you must tell-a the public."

I assured him I would.

That night I made my own "debut" in front of the great gold curtain, coming out to announce the cast changes. Of course I was greeted with grumblings that echoed around the house; I even heard a few boos. I held up my hand to quiet everyone and then spoke about our disappointment in Freni's cancellation and our gratitude to Miss Scotto for stepping in. I went on to explain that the vagaries of opera life are such that Nicolai Gedda was forced to cancel because of the flu. The audience became restless; I could see people looking at each other, shaking their heads in disgust. I held up my hand again and said, "Replacing Mr. Gedda tonight will be Luciano Pavarotti!"

The roar of sound was instantaneous, like a sudden event in a great sports arena. Cheers, bravos, whistles, feet stomping—all could be plainly heard behind the curtain as I stepped backstage.

Pavarotti was sitting at the little table, stage center in the Act I set of the production, waiting in place for the opera to begin and listening to the continuing audience reaction to my news. I went over, placing one hand on his shoulder and gesturing toward the auditorium with the other, and asked if that furor was all right.

He listened to the ovation for a moment longer, then, smiling, turned to me and said: "That's-a nice!!"

Later that same year Pavarotti returned for his regular Met season, singing with Joan Sutherland in the famous *La Fille du Régiment* where he snapped off those nine high C's in the famous second-act aria. New York went wild; it was not only the vocal feat, it was also the elegance and musicality with which the music was delivered. Here were Sutherland and Pavarotti at their prime, having a good time together onstage and poking a little fun at themselves in a bit of self-parody. For those who heard them, it was unforgettable.

Pavarotti is a warm, caring personality. To know him, one must start with an important point in his background: he came from a poor but loving family. Born in Modena, Italy, in 1935 to parents who were music lovers, his father, a baker of bread, had a fine, untrained voice and was delighted when his son showed promise as a singer. He first studied singing with Arrigo Pola, then with Ettore Campogalliani. His official career began in 1961, when he won a competition at the Teatro Reggio Emilia and made his debut there as Rodolfo. He was then getting fifty dollars a performance. The following year he sang in Amsterdam and at Covent Garden, where he met Joan Sutherland.

By 1965 he was the leading tenor in Sutherland's own production of *Lucia,* a company she organized to tour Australia. As he himself says, he learned a great deal from her. "How is it possible that this woman's notes never seem to end? How does she produce this endless chain of sound?" He imitated the Sutherland technique and has paid full tribute to her, saying it was she who taught him how to breathe correctly.

Pavarotti has great affection for the Metropolitan Opera and this was never more evident than during the Met's first tour of Japan in the spring of 1975. For reasons unknown, that particular spring was a difficult one in the history of Japanese-American relations, but I had no idea of this until we arrived in Tokyo and discovered our performances there and elsewhere in the country were by no means sold out. Here we had a roster that in addition to Pavarotti, Corelli, and James McCracken included Sutherland, Marilyn Horne, Dorothy Kirsten, Robert Merrill, and other splendid artists in performances of *Carmen, La Traviata* and *La Bohème*. Usually such star names sold out immediately; Japan was then and continues to be one of the world's largest markets for Western classical music. All of our stars had huge record sales attesting to this fact. For some reason, however, our tickets were very slow to move.

Our Japanese hosts, the Chibbu-Nippon Company of Nagoya, were polite but noncommittal. It took a couple of days before I was able to see an old friend, Bernard Krisher, a longtime resident of Japan who was then *Newsweek*'s chief correspondent in that part of the world. Krisher explained that when the Japanese feel pressured by the United States, they occasionally show their disappointment by a subtle but unspoken boycott of things American, especially something as high culture as the Metropolitan. Krisher's comments were echoed by a Japanese friend, Akio Morita, chairman of Sony, a skilled businessman with wide contacts in the West, who suggested we overcome our problems by appearing on NHK, the government television network, with one of our productions. He also warned me about a television program on which I was already scheduled to appear, a popular interview show much like "Today" in the United States.

"The program wants to embarrass the Metropolitan," he said. "Be careful. The questions may sound innocent, but they will be slanted and disagreeable."

I remembered his words when Marilyn Horne, the conductor Henry Lewis, Pavarotti, and I assembled in a studio to tape the program. The questions asked by the host and translated by a slim, beautiful, low-voiced female interpreter did sound simple enough, but as a precaution I asked Pavarotti if he would speak for the Metropolitan. I just had time to pull him aside and whisper Morita's warning in his ear before the tape machines were whirring.

When the first question about the Metropolitan was addressed to me, I replied I thought it would be more appropriate for an artist to answer, since the company was, and

LUCIANO PAVAROTTI

New York City
February 25, 1992

He could allot only ten minutes. I was to have my lights arranged in the ballroom of the Hampshire House and there wait—what turned out to be five hours—for Pavarotti to come down from his suite to be photographed. But in comparison to two years of being told by his manager, "We will find a time," in response to my requests for a sitting, five hours now seemed like seconds. Pavarotti entered the ballroom wearing an oversize beret, looking more like Holbein's painting of Henry VIII than Luciano Pavarotti. He sat and I began shooting, frame by frame, carefully changing my lighting and the angle of view. "Taking one peec-ture like moving mountain," Luciano said as I switched lenses. "Why not take lots and lots of peec-ture with no stop?!" "Trust me, Luciano," I answered. To which he retorted: "My friend, I trust-a no man. You trust-a me, you get good peec-ture." "Yes, let me just look through this lens," I said. And before he could do his routine expressions—forced looks he would give to the camera—I tripped the shutter. —J.D.R.

always will be, a company of artists. I turned to Pavarotti and said, "Mr. Pavarotti, perhaps you might explain about the Metropolitan Opera?"

With that he was off and running. In wonderfully accented English he explained the history of the Met, its great singers and conductors, its relationship to other opera companies around the world, its worldwide reputation. After the general portrait, he spoke about the great Enrico Caruso and the Met's key role in developing his career. The more he talked, the more emotional he became. By the time he was finished, I wanted to jump up and salute the flag. As he concluded, he looked at the host in a manner that was quite plain: don't tramp on me or the Metropolitan. While the cameras cut away from him, he turned his head slightly toward me and winked.

When the program was over, he asked me if he'd been all right. I told him I only wished I'd recorded his remarks; they were the best promotion for the Metropolitan I'd ever heard. He was not displeased.

Morita saw the broadcast and called to congratulate Pavarotti and reiterate to me that our problems would only be finally solved if the company gave a full performance on NHK. The difficulty with this idea was that we had a clear understanding with our unions that there would be no television. Nonetheless, I called the company together and explained, as best I could, the odd political-emotional

climate we were facing and asked if they would allow a television taping of *La Traviata.* Sutherland and Pavarotti cleared everything with their other star colleagues, and much to my surprise, everyone else agreed as well. We went on the air at 8:00 P.M. on a Sunday night over the full NHK network and literally the next day there was not a ticket to be had for any of our performances in Tokyo, Nagoya, or Osaka. Pavarotti had set the stage; the company on television was its own best answer to the implied boycott. The music lovers of Japan responded.

Pavarotti is now a household name across the world, even with people who can't tell the difference between *Aïda* and *La Bohème.* He has succeeded in touching millions of people through his performances, recordings, television appearances, films, books, and personal appearances.

My favorite statement about him is one he made about himself to a reporter:

The pleasure of the profession is the human warmth around me, the public out there. I always had this, even before I was a singer. As a child too, I was the same—I was never home but at other houses always talking and joking. My life is full of people, generally good friends. I decide to spend my life with friends. I am a singer of success, and I'm enthusiastic of the job I do and enthusiastic of life. I love people. This is an incredible and beautiful thing in life, to be kissed by God. If I am kissed by God, I thank him by doing my best. After the performance, the most beautiful thing is to remain one hour after to talk. These people come from all over and they are in love with the art of Luciano Pavarotti.

Someone once wrote that his voice is like pure Italian sunshine. I agree, and knowing him as I do, I'd add from my own personal experiences that his soul is as well.

Placido Domingo

lacido Domingo and I began working together in 1970, when I engaged him as Corelli's standby for a performance and videotaping of the Verdi *Requiem* in London under the baton of Leonard Bernstein. The two of us had tea together one afternoon in New York to settle the details of the engagement, and within minutes I knew I had an unhappy man on my hands.

"Why don't you just engage me?" he asked. "The *Requiem* is one of my favorite works. I want the privilege of working with Maestro Bernstein. I cannot spend my life in Corelli's shadow."

I explained that contracts had already been signed, and that I wasn't trying to insult him by asking his cooperation but had come at the urging of the maestro, who also hoped they might work together on other projects.

After a long conversation he agreed to reserve the *Requiem* time for us if I contacted him no later than three days before the first performance. I did, of course, the moment Corelli announced his expected cancellation, and we began an association that not only included the *Requiem* but also a gala film of Beethoven's Ninth Symphony with Bernstein and the Vienna Philharmonic celebrating the composer's two hundredth birthday. Not surprisingly our association also continued during my years at the Met.

PLACIDO DOMINGO

New York City
April 11, 1992

His name means "peaceful Sunday," an irony to an unremitting schedule: when he is not singing, Domingo is likely to be found on the podium or engaged in council as an arts administrator. Only a brief interval of time could be managed for a sitting, and complex arrangements had to be made for me to photograph Domingo in his dressing room at the Met; he would be singing the Saturday afternoon radio broadcast of *La Fanciulla del West* and agreed to sit following wardrobe prior to his first act entrance on stage. In those minutes usually reserved for composure, Domingo gave me his total concentration regardless that his voice was about to be heard nationwide. *Gracious* is the word for Domingo.

—J.D.R.

Domingo is an unusual artist. In addition to being a splendid singer, he is an all-around musician—an expert pianist and a fine conductor. Over the years he has built an immense repertoire, ranging from lyric roles to Otello. He is a fast study and a complete professional who gets on well both with his colleagues and arts administrators.

His early training took place in Mexico, where his family moved from Spain when Placido was a little boy. Both his parents were singers specializing in Spanish operettas known as *zarzuelas.* The story is that Mrs. Domingo came home from a performance one night and gave birth that same night to her son.

As a boy Placido studied the piano, and as a young man, he studied conducting with Igor Markevich. At sixteen he discovered he had a voice and started as a baritone, singing and playing the piano in nightclubs, and also appearing occasionally in his parents' *zarzuelas.* At sixteen he also got married; he once told me most of his adolescence was spent in constant biological conflict with the Catholic church. The marriage didn't last, but they had a son who, not too long ago, made Placido one of the youngest grandfathers in the history of opera.

For a while he studied singing with Carlo Morelli and later with Franco Iglesias.

After marrying a second time, he and his bride Marta, also a singer, joined the Israeli Opera where, now a tenor, he began to have technical problems. He was constantly cracking on high notes, to the point where he was ready to give up singing. Iglesias, who had accompanied the young Domingos to Israel, worked on diaphragm support and finally managed to free his voice to develop into the one we know today—strong, clear, well-focused, and dependable.

He has always been a musical singer who looked for more than just golden sounds. "Singers," he once told an interviewer, "can be musicians and not know music. Conductors can know all the music in the world but have no feeling for music because they are intellectual, analytical. I do not like to hear a musically well-trained singer who makes me feel they are singing on a dotted note. It is the *line* of singing, with the dots and legato and staccato. To make music you have to go beyond all these things."

Even with that splendid vocal definition, however, he occasionally finds a familiar role becoming too treacherous to continue in his repertoire. Such was the case with Manrico in *Il Trovatore*, the work which in 1973–1974 opened my second season as general manager of the Metropolitan.

In addition to Domingo, the cast included Martina Arroyo, Cornell MacNeill, John Macurdy, and Mignon Dunn. The conductor was James Levine. The production was well received by the critics and public alike, and I was therefore surprised one afternoon, before an evening performance, when Domingo appeared in my office in great agitation.

"You must let me out of the performance tonight," he began. "I cannot face Manrico anymore. *'Di quella pira'* is too treacherous for me. I'm afraid of it."

My first reaction was that he was teasing, but that feeling lasted only a moment. As I watched in amazement, he sank to his knees and, clasping his hands together, began to pray at me.

"Please!" he begged. "Let me cancel tonight. I can't face that aria again."

I confess this was a new experience. I was becoming accustomed to tenorial tensions, but until this moment no one had ever addressed me as a priest. I leaned down to lift him up, but he'd wrapped his hands around my ankles and refused to move.

"Come on, Placido," I heard myself say. "It's really not that bad."

"Oh, yes it is," he managed to choke out. "You don't know. I cannot sing anymore." I thought I saw tears in his eyes.

The idea of allowing him to cancel under these particular circumstances seemed absurd, yet obviously he was in terror and something had to be done.

I asked whether the entire role panicked him or just *'Di quella pira.'* He answered that he was unconcerned about the rest of the part. An idea was needed: how to make it possible for him to sing the role up to the aria and again at the aria's conclusion. Eliminating *"Di quella pira"* was out of the question. The only possibility was to have another tenor sing it. But who? And how?

I checked our roster and discovered that William Lewis was Placido's cover. Lewis is one of those artists vital to the Met's artistic success. A sturdy and reliable singer in his own right, he had the interests of the company very much in mind.

"I've a thought," I said to Placido, who by now was sitting anxiously in a chair before me. "What if Bill Lewis were to sing the aria and you simply mime it?"

He looked at me quizzically.

"I'll have to ask Bill, of course, but I think we could hide him in the orchestra pit and somehow get him to sing if you really feel the need."

I could see waves of relief pass across his face.

"That's wonderful," he said. "I feel much better. You arrange everything and tell me what I'm to do."

I telephoned Lewis and explained the situation. He was, not unexpectedly, surprised by my odd request, but after conferring with James Levine he accepted the challenge.

We decided to dress him in a black pullover and seat him in the woodwind section of the orchestra with his head directly under the feet of the prompter. I told Placido that when the orchestral introduction to *"Di quella pira"* began, if he felt he couldn't sing he was to look straight down at the prompter and nod his head. The prompter, in turn, would tap on Lewis's shoulders.

I went to Placido's dressing room just before the performance and gave him his instructions.

"Okay, fine," he said. "I'm all ready and shall mime carefully. Maybe the audience will never know."

When I took my seat and scanned the orchestra, I spotted Lewis parked between two woodwind players. If anyone noticed him at all, he would be taken for a second oboe or third clarinet. This was one time when I blessed the orchestra's anonymity.

The opera proceeded in splendid form and presently I heard the aria's familiar introductory passages. Placido moved himself directly in front of the prompter; I looked up at him and down at Lewis.

Suddenly *"Di quella pira, l'orendo foco"* rang out in fine style, unmistakably Domingo's voice—steady, clear, strong, powerful. I listened in astonishment; the audience screamed its approval. I looked down at Lewis, who was smiling, either from relief or knowing he'd made a powerful psychological contribution to the evening. He'd been Placido's security blanket. As far as I've been able to determine, Domingo never sang Manrico again.

These days Placido Domingo might be called the marathon man of opera. In some thirty years he has sung more performances than most singers do in a lifetime. He is a dominant force in the record market and has made more television appearances in opera than any other singer of his day. He wants to reach people, "to be known by many people in my own time," as he himself says, and he keeps running, defying the doomsayers who continue to anguish that he will burn himself out.

To his singing schedule he has now added regular appearances as a conductor. He's also trying more vocal concerts, something he shied away from for years, and he would like to promote *zarzuelas* and Latin American music everywhere.

Knowing him, I suspect whatever else he decides for the future, he will always have his desire to bring happiness, excitement, and love to his public.

And they will return those feelings.

Martti Talvela

T he late—and great—Martti Talvela was the only person who ever made my office at the Metropolitan Opera seem like a puppy kennel. He was, after all, six feet seven inches tall and must have weighed well over two hundred and fifty pounds, but like those wonderful "rough but oh, so tender" ads for Champion spark plugs, he was a gentle giant. When we shook hands, mine disappeared entirely into his.

We first met in 1973, when August Everding, the opera stage director, brought him to my office for a meeting about *Boris Godunov.* We were planning a new production of this masterpiece, based on Mussorgsky's own revised 1872 score rather than the reworkings of either Rimsky-Korsakov or Shostakovich. Talvela was one of the few major bassos who agreed to sing this version, which does not end in the death of Boris but with the Simpleton, alone onstage, singing about the ageless woes and tribulations of Mother Russia.

At the meeting, which included the designer, Ming Cho Lee, and the conductor,

Thomas Schippers, I stressed that we had to find a way of avoiding the usual long waits between the opera's many scenes, waits that inevitably break the plot tension and always bring the action to a dead halt. "It is, after all, one continuous story line about the Russian people," I reminded everyone.

There were nods of agreement around the room as Ming Cho Lee, taking an unlined pad out of his briefcase, began making sketches.

MARTTI TALVELA

New York City
March 4, 1987

I began to make up his face when he interrupted, saying: "If you want my soul you should photograph my face clean; otherwise it will not be who I am." I wet the sponge and removed all traces of makeup.

—J.D.R.

Talvela made some interesting historical observations, stemming from his extensive research into the character of Boris. He also reminded everyone that as a Finn, he knew something about Russian attitudes from the love/hate relationship the Finns have always had for their imposing neighbor. He was especially helpful to Ming, who, after a number of conversations, did indeed find the right design solutions to make the production a dramatic as well as musical success. The production continues to be presented at the Metropolitan to this day.

Martti Talvela was born into an ancient farming family in the eastern Finland province of Karelia. After his general studies, he qualified as a schoolteacher, but with his fine natural voice was persuaded by family and friends to take singing lessons. In 1960 he entered a national lieder competition and won. From that moment on, singing became his life's work.

Having successfully talked his way into the National Opera in Helsinki, he quickly decided it would be best to leave Finland for further study in Sweden. His progress was so rapid that Set Svanholm, then general director of the Stockholm Royal Opera, offered him an opportunity for his first role—Sparafucile in *Rigoletto* in 1961.

Once on the operatic road, he rarely faltered. In 1962 Wieland Wagner invited him to the Bayreuth Festival to sing Titurel. That won him a contract with the Deutsche

Oper in Berlin, which led to his La Scala debut as the Grand Inquisitor in *Don Carlos.*

Talvela always credited his stage successes to Berlin, where the Oper's music director, Lorin Maazel, worked closely with him. From what became his new home base, he soon began making guest appearances in all the leading German opera houses, and by the midsixties was frequently singing in Milan, Rome, Vienna, Paris, and London. In the late sixties his career spread to the United States, where he sang first in San Francisco and then, in 1968, at the Met, debuting as the Grand Inquisitor.

Six years later he reappeared as Boris. His performance was awesome—vocally secure and dramatically passionate. We surrounded him with a splendid cast—Paul Plishka as Pimen; Harry Theyard, the false Dimitri; Donald Gramm, Varlaam; Andrea Velis, the Simpleton; and as the Polish Princess, Marina, Mignon Dunn. George Ballanchine returned to the Met to choreograph the Polish scene in the second act; Ming Cho Lee gave us a stunning production, Everding brilliant direction, and Schippers one of the finest musical performances of his all-too-short career.

But Boris was the centerpiece of the evening, and here Talvela used his great size to advantage, a splendid example of careful underacting, of letting body and face carry the messages. He knew what he was doing every moment on the stage. By the time he toppled from his throne in the death scene, the crash was horrifying. He ended up lying on the stage sprawled and twisted, with great glassy eyes staring at the audience, the picture of total collapse.

The premiere itself turned out to be an overall glorious event. At the end of the opera, the audience leapt to its collective feet, cheering, shouting, and yelling bravos. I finally had to close off the applause by ordering the iron curtain lowered to prevent overtime, but not before Talvela's solo curtain calls, where he was showered with the highest honor an opera audience can bestow: confetti made from torn-up house programs.

Before the first performance, Talvela presented me with a massive Finnish crystal vase as an opening night present, a vase big enough for two bottles of champagne. It is a splendid souvenir of this unusual, sensitive man who died so much before his time.

Sherrill Milnes

One of the pleasures of my years at the Metropolitan Opera was presenting, for the first time, Sherrill Milnes as Don Giovanni, a role he's now made his own. Goeran Gentele, having heard Sherrill in a variety of Verdi roles, felt it was time he came to grips with the Don and offered him a new production of the opera for the 1973–1974 season. Sherrill accepted, but with some nervousness. Gentele told him not to worry; they would work together preparing the role. Shortly after their understanding, however, Gentele was killed, and because of financial restrictions, I was forced to cancel the new *Don Giovanni* in favor of reviving the old 1957 Eugene Berman classic.

Sherrill was extremely upset and wanted to bow out. He indicated his feelings to me one night in Minneapolis during the Met's 1972 spring tour; I suggested we breakfast the next morning to talk things over.

Now, it was my custom to travel on the Met tour with my wife, a custom welcomed by our hosts in tour cities. I shared Sherrill's conversation with her and mentioned that we were going to discuss matters over breakfast. Rather gently, she asked if she might join us. I frowned a bit at this idea, suggesting it might be better if we continued our informal arrangement of keeping a wide separation between "church" and "state." However, I knew she was particularly fond of Sherrill and well aware of the importance to me of his keeping the Don Giovanni commitment.

SHERRILL MILNES

New York City
September 26, 1986

I asked Sherrill if he could sum up his feelings—the experience—on what it is to receive an ovation. He went to his desk and, with careful thought, wrote these words: "Macbeth, Iago, Rigoletto, Simon Boccanegra—these are the roles that make you feel like you're laying your life out before the public. These are what give you satisfaction. When you are applauded for them you feel both enormous excitement and great humility—and sometimes I cry." —J.D.R.

The next morning over his breakfast coffee, Sherrill began laying out the reasons he wished to quit. As he talked I realized what was at the bottom of his problem: with Gentele gone, who was going to coach him in the role? As this thought entered my mind, I heard my wife say to him: "Why don't you ask George London? I'll bet he'd be delighted with the idea." I looked at her with gratitude. Sherrill smiled too, but quickly became crestfallen. "George London was the best Don Giovanni I ever saw or heard," he commented, "but I've never met him." "Well, fortunately I know him very well," I replied. "Years ago I produced some of his recordings. I'll be happy to ask him." Sherrill beamed. "If you can arrange for me to work with him, I'll stay with the part." We all shook hands.

After breakfast I put in a call to George London, then artistic director of the Kennedy Center in Washington, D.C. When I explained my reason for calling, there was a long pause before he answered by saying he thought Sherrill Milnes had the potential to be the best Don of his generation, if he was willing to work hard. "Have him get in touch with me this afternoon," George concluded. I relayed the good news to Sherrill, who promptly called. The two began working together immediately.

And so it was that on the evening of March 28, 1974, Sherrill Milnes sang his first

Don, surrounded by a formidable cast including Leontyne Price as Donna Anna, Teresa Zylis-Gara as Donna Elvira, Stuart Burrows as Don Ottavio, Walter Berry as Leporello, Teresa Stratas as Zerlina, Raymond Michalski as Masetto, James Morris as the Commendatore, and James Levine conducting his first Mozart opera at the Met.

Sherrill made opera history that night with his magnificent acting and singing. George London, watching backstage, tears streaming down his cheeks, realized he'd successfully passed on his mantel to a splendid younger artist.

These days Sherrill Milnes graces the world as the all-American baritone, the latest in a grand line that includes Lawrence Tibbett, John Charles Thomas, Leonard Warren, Robert Merrill, and George London. Milnes's voice is big and burly, like his physical frame. He exudes sexuality, a machismo that is undeniable, and in so doing commands the stage with a swagger and authority. For the most part he has specialized in Verdi, slowly building his repertoire of those formidable parts that range from princes and counts and doges to jesters and bourgeois fathers.

George Bernard Shaw, in his music-critic days, once complained that Verdi kept the baritone voice "banging away" at the top third of the range. I think that's where Milnes's strength lies. With the strongest of Otellos, Milnes as Iago can hold his own in the thundering *"Si pel ciel"* that brings down the curtain on Act II. His brilliant cabaletta as Miller in Act I of *Luisa Miller* literally made him a star at the Met in late 1960s. Since then he has put his unique mark on the vast Verdi repertoire: *Macbeth, Ernani, I Vespri Siciliani, Rigoletto, La Traviata, Don Carlo, Un Ballo in Maschera, Il Trovatore, Aïda, La Forza del Destino, Simon Boccanegra,* to say nothing of his non-Verdi roles in *I Pagliacci, Andrea Chenier, Pique Dame, Eugene Onegin, Lohengrin, Das Rheingold,* and, of course, *Don Giovanni.*

All those noble, troubled, or besieged figures are a long way from the Illinois farm where Sherrill was born. His mother, a singer, pianist, choir director, and conductor, had always been active in her community, teaching voice as well as leading the choir. Sherrill took a crack at both the violin and piano before settling on singing, and first at Drake University and later at Northwestern University, he began serious work, joining Margaret

Hillis's Chicago Symphony Chorus. He was also teaching school, doing radio commercials, and singing in opera workshops. Those workshop performances led to Boris Goldovsky's touring company—fifty-three Masettos in *Don Giovanni* on tour. In 1961 he debuted with Rosa Ponselle's Baltimore Civic Opera as Gerard in *Andrea Chenier*. This, in turn, led to Pittsburgh, San Antonio, Houston, Cincinnati, and a European debut in Milan at the Teatro Nuovo in *Il Barbière di Siviglia*. Milan was hotly followed by his first New York City Opera performances as Valentin in *Faust*, followed by Figaro and the elder Germont. Then 1965 brought him to the Metropolitan in *Faust* and from then on he has literally reigned as *el supremo* in the baritone slot.

Sherrill is conscious of his image, of building it and touching his audience. He keeps in first-class physical condition with a gym in his apartment. He looks and acts the role of the dashing hero and feels the whole idea of opera being accessible to only the privileged few is nonsense. "Music is primarily emotional, not intellectual," he once said. "You don't have to have a degree to understand it; you can just let it wash over you, and your body will respond. Communication is the whole thing."

And Sherrill Milnes communicates.

James Morris

very impresario should have at least one moment when that title is fully defined by an opportunity to play a crucial role in forwarding a career. I've been fortunate that over the years this has happened to me several times, but none more exciting than on January 15, 1975, when I sat at the first Metropolitan performance of James Morris as Don Giovanni, a role he had "covered" the previous season for Sherrill Milnes.

Watching and listening to Morris that night as he sang and acted the Don with vocal power and compelling masculinity, I was witnessing this young artist take his first major step from being a reliable *comprimàrio* to being an international star, a position he has now brought to shining perfection as the leading Wagnerian bass of his generation.

The genesis was simple: In the fall of 1971, when I arrived at the Met to begin my observation year, I attended an October performance of *Rigoletto*. I've totally forgotten who sang Rigoletto or Gilda or the Duke—they were undoubtedly splendid—but the first appearance of Sparafucile made me rustle through my program to find out who the artist was. There onstage was the physical personification of sleaziness coupled with a vibrant voice that, quite literally, sent shivers down my spine. I knew instantly I was hearing a young man destined for a major career.

After the performance I went back and introduced myself to what turned out to be a big, gangly all-American kid, who smiled shyly and thanked me for my comments. I was surprised that his speaking voice had almost the same resonance as his singing voice, and was delighted that his laugh was loud and full.

James Morris—or Jimmy, as his friends call him—made his Met debut in 1971 as the King in *Aïda,* quickly becoming the nonpareil bass-baritone *comprimàrio,* the kind of artist about whom opera managers dream. In short order he was singing Monterone in *Rigoletto,* the Marquis of Calatrava in *La Forza del Destino,* Samuele in *Un Ballo in Maschera* and the Friar in *Don Carlo.* He also sang a soldier in *Salome,* Zuniga on the Met tour, and Raimondo in *Lucia* for students. He was indispensable.

Jimmy grew up in Baltimore, where he studied voice all through high school. Opera didn't interest him much at that time, but after he sang *"Eri tu,"* the big aria from *La Forza del Destino,* and found out what the words meant, he suddenly stopped switching radio stations every time opera came on the air. He spent one year at the University of Maryland living the fraternity life before transferring to the Peabody Conservatory, where the curriculum was more to the point. Frank Valentino taught him there for two years, and Nicola Moscona at Philadelphia's Academy of Vocal Arts taught him for three years, but Rosa Ponselle got to him first. She came out of retirement to teach him repertory when he was fresh out of high school, almost before he even knew how to sing. All she had to hear was the voice and she knew.

About Ponselle, Jimmy has this to say: "When I was in Peabody, Miss Ponselle was instrumental in getting me into the Baltimore Opera Company, and many roles I did with them I coached with her. Was she good? She was fabulous. She taught me about interpreting—the emotion, the word, the role, the other characters onstage. I was getting my vocal instruction from others, but she contributed a great deal to the vocal technique."

At the age of twenty-three, during his third year in Philadelphia, he was pronounced ready to audition for the Met. Again his own words:

> I've been extremely fortunate with the friends I've made in this profession. One in particular comes to mind, my voice teacher Nicola Moscona. On the day of my Metropolitan Opera audition, I was extremely nervous and, after throwing up my breakfast, I telephoned him. He said, "Stay right there—I come take you and a paper bag to the Met." Later onstage, I had sung one aria and when the people present asked for a second aria, my mind went totally blank. After standing there like an idiot for what seemed at least an hour, I heard this fierce whisper from the wings— "Simone, *stupido,* Simone!" I sang the bass aria from *Simone Boccanegra* and was asked to join the Metropolitan Opera.

It wasn't long after I became general manager that the conductor, Max Rudolf, suggested that Morris was ready for bigger things and asked what I thought of his covering (understudying) Sherrill Milnes's first performances as the Don. I thought the idea splendid and suggested it to Jimmy, who hesitated a bit at first but then decided he was ready to prepare the role.

In a season that kept him busy with all kinds of *comprimàrio* parts in both Italian and German repertoires, I forgot to ask how his Don preparations were going until one night, just as I was getting ready to leave the opera house, he asked to see me. When he came to my office he was extremely—and uncharacteristically—nervous about something.

We went across the street to a French restaurant where my wife was waiting for me. Betty and I both liked this refreshingly vibrant young fellow, only a year older than our eldest son, and as he sat down we exchanged glances, knowing something was wrong. Finally he got around to blurting out his problem—he'd been offered an opportunity to sing Don Giovanni in a performance at Chautauqua and to do this he needed to be excused from the Met spring tour. Could he have the time off?

That was not an easy question to answer. He was such a vital part of the company that to replace him in all his roles was a real puzzle. But the more I thought about the opportunity, the more I realized it was just what he needed. Even without consulting my colleagues I felt that psychologically he needed to have a quick, affirmative response from me. I told him he could. His eyes filled with tears as he extended both hands to thank me.

JAMES MORRIS

New York City
October 19, 1987

When I photographed James Morris he was on the verge of being lauded one of the foremost Wagnerian bassos of our time—if not *the* definitive Wotan for all time. Already he had received acclaim on the Ringstrasse as the *Walküre* Wotan, but had yet to sing his now-historic triple *Ring*. As we worked, he analyzed Wagner's three Wotans and concluded that the *Walküre* Wotan "is the most human of the three, torn between what his heart tells him to do and what he feels bound to do." Morris gradually became introspective as he spoke, gazing into space— Wotan absorbed in contemplation.

—J.D.R.

My decision turned out to be a godsend all around. Sherrill Milnes never missed a performance of the Don during his 1973–1974 season, but in 1974–1975, Roger Soyer, the French artist scheduled to replace him, became ill and canceled his Met contract. That gave me the opportunity to offer the role to Jimmy, who seized the chance and, as I've already indicated, took off for stardom.

Two other people were also captivated by his Don—Joan Sutherland and Richard Bonynge. Bonynge suggested that Morris's next major role ought to be Sir Giorgio in the 1976 production we were planning of *I Puritani*. The cast already included Joan, Pavarotti, and Sherrill Milnes. The addition of Morris made this the finest quartet of singers assembled for this opera in modern times. The opening night audience went into happy hysterics.

One of my last projects at the Met also involved James Morris. When John Dexter began planning Benjamin Britten's *Billy Budd,* he and I both felt that Morris was the only person to play Claggart. Dexter's idea of the role was to focus on good versus evil, that Claggart and Billy should be the same age and handsomeness, like reverse sides of the same coin.

Jimmy arrived as a singing actor with Claggart. Andrew Porter, writing in *The New Yorker,* caught his impact: "the first Claggart of my experience to express fully the Lucifer-like beauty, sorrow, and passion of the Evil One and to embody the occasional hint that in Billy and Claggart we have a final projection of the twinned bright and dark angels . . . who recur in Melville's work."

These days I watch Jimmy Morris's rise in the opera world with almost parental pride. Listening to him sing and act as the foremost Wotan alive gives me a special pleasure. He is still an oversize cowboy at heart, but his booming bass and stage presence bring life and pleasure to countless people all over the world.

Again his own words:

Opera provides wonderful chances for escapism. An opera singer can be a peasant one day, royalty the next. One time a father, the next a lover. One day God, and the next the Devil himself. What other career, other than an actor, provides for such a varied life? But with opera you have the added dimension of music.

Many people think the life of an opera singer is very glamorous. Sometimes it is, but there is also another side. The constant traveling, one hotel room after another, long periods of separation from family and friends, constantly feeling like you are in school with the continuous learning of new repertoire and the relearning of previously performed roles. But when you are onstage performing the great masterpieces and accompanied by wonderful orchestras, it all seems to come together and at that moment you have your reward.

In a very real sense, James Morris is one of the rewards of my side of the profession.

And Other Friends

Isaac Stern

$\textit{I}$ would probably never have been offered a position at the Met if it hadn't been for Isaac Stern. In the 1960s, during my time as programming officer for Lincoln Center, Isaac insisted that I meet his friend Goeran Gentele, the intendant of the Royal Opera, Stockholm. He didn't just suggest a meeting; he orchestrated it.

At the time, I was organizing visits from European performing groups, including opera companies, to participate in a series of summer festivals. Negotiations were in various stages with La Scala, Rome, Covent Garden, and Prague when it occurred to Isaac that the Royal Opera, Stockholm, might make a splendid addition.

Now, when Isaac Stern seizes on an idea, and that idea passes overnight inspection, he is clever, insistent, and passionately stubborn about carrying it out.

First came the telephone calls from around the world, then the messages, often delivered by mutual friends as they passed through New York, and finally, on a cold winter afternoon in 1966, the long visit over tea and drinks at our apartment. At the end of that occasion I knew my next trip abroad was bound to include Stockholm.

As it turned out, I had to go to Stockholm quite unexpectedly; a problem for the 1967 festival made it necessary to meet and consult Gentele, and armed with a letter of introduction from Isaac, I arrived in that dark, winter-bound city on an early March afternoon about five weeks after Stern's and my conversation.

Gentele and I met, discussed our business, and relaxed into a conversation about our mutual friend. That, in turn, led to dinner, where I met his glamorous wife, Marit, heard a superb performance of *Tristan und Isolde* in his opera house, and eventually developed a friendship that also became a professional operatic association lasting until July 1972, when his shocking death propelled me into the world operatic spotlight as his successor.

Isaac sensed early on that Gentele and I had much in common; he was right. To me this was just another example of the Stern understanding and subtlety about people, something I've observed over many years of friendship.

I'll never forget the first time I met him. It was in the spring of 1953, at the beginning of my career in the performing arts. I was on my first professional assignment as tour manager for Jascha Heifetz, and in April, after several long and lonely months on the road, I was back in New York, where Heifetz was to play with the New York Philharmonic, and I had a chance to rejoin my family.

One afternoon I was invited by the pianist Eugene Istomin for a drink, and when I arrived I immediately recognized the stocky figure curled up in an armchair. Our friendship began when he pulled himself up and moved across the room to shake hands.

"I'm so sorry," he murmured, "what a terrible business. You must be upset."

"What terrible business?" I asked. He looked solemn and sympathetic.

"You know, about Jascha," he replied.

"What about Jascha?" I asked.

"I'm so very sorry," he said again, softly this time, with sad eyes accompanying his voice. He looked at me for a moment, placing a comforting hand on my shoulder.

By this time I was beginning to sweat, even though Istomin's apartment was quite cold. "What are you talking about?" I asked, anxiety written all over my face.

"You know, about his fiddle and the accident."

By now I was thoroughly confused; I'd just left the great man at his hotel, his fiddle case, as always, firmly clasped in his right hand.

"That beautiful Guarnerius," he went on, shaking his head, "such a shame."

I stared at him for a moment and then, quite suddenly, I realized he was pulling my leg. "Oh, that old thing. Well, it's falling apart anyway and he needs a new one. I wouldn't worry, if I were you!" We both laughed. "You had me there for a moment, Mr. Stern. I suppose this is violin humor?"

"You might call it envy," he said. "You're working with the very best. And my name's Isaac."

It was only a short time after that initial meeting that we began working together. In 1959 I was invited to head the Masterworks department of Columbia Records. Stern was and still is under exclusive contract to Columbia Masterworks, now known as Sony Classical. At the beginning of our association, however, I thought my previous years with Heifetz might make him a little suspicious of my musical loyalties, but that was not the case. I quickly discovered he was welcoming to all his colleagues, a spoken generosity that was always turned into action. We plunged immediately into record planning for the next several seasons, including concerti with Bernstein and the New York Philharmonic, Ormandy and the Philadelphia Orchestra, Szell and the Cleveland Orchestra, and solo repertoire with his longtime accompanist, Alexander Zakin. It was not the actual recordings that sharpened our personal friendship, however, although those proceeded in an exciting and rewarding manner; it was Stern the concerned citizen.

During the mid-1950s, New York City had gone through one of its periodic up-and-down real estate cycles, but by 1959 the market was booming again. The charm and variety of New York's architecture was fast disappearing in favor of faceless concrete slabs and acres of unsmiling glass. One site earmarked by developers was Carnegie Hall. The fact that the building was one of the world's most famous concert halls mattered not a whit. The owners, fearful of competition from a new cultural center being built in the scrubby Lincoln Square area of Manhattan's west side, decided the old building should be replaced by an office tower. The fact that Carnegie Hall's most important tenant, the New

York Philharmonic, was to have its own home in the new center pushed development plans ahead faster than otherwise might have been expected. Suddenly newspapers were carrying stories that the Hall would be replaced by a red-slabbed skyscraper. There were, not unexpectedly, cries of anguish from the music world, but these were soon lost in the hyperbole about the new Lincoln Center project. Only two voices kept up a vigorous protest: one was the impresario Sol Hurok, the other, Isaac Stern.

With characteristic energy, Isaac and his wife, Vera, began a campaign to save Carnegie Hall. In short order they rallied Robert Wagner, then New York's mayor, and a major group of state political figures, including Governor Nelson Rockefeller and the leaders of the state legislature, plus an important philanthropist, J. M. Kaplan, countless artists and concerned citizens, and the support of the *New York Times.* All this activity resulted in an enabling bill, passed by the legislature and signed by the governor, authorizing the City of New York to purchase the hall and lease it to a nonprofit corporation. Stern became president of the new organization and still is. He succeeded then, as he has succeeded to this day, in drawing around him leading business, educational, political, artistic, and legal leaders to serve on the boards of one or the other of the organization's two operating units: the Carnegie Hall Corporation and the Carnegie Hall Society.

Of course, while this civic activity was going on Stern was also continuing his career. At one point, early in 1961, we found ourselves together in Paris, where he was to give concerts and make some recordings. I arrived a few days before him to set up the necessary studio details, and we arranged to rendezvous early one evening at his hotel. When I arrived at his suite, the living room was filled with a large assortment of his friends babbling away in several languages. The bathroom door was ajar; Isaac was soaking in the tub, a cigar clenched between his teeth, answering questions or making comments. When he spotted me he called out introductions in French, Russian, and English. I shook hands all around, and moments later he emerged into the room, barefoot and wrapped in a large towel, and offered me a drink from the well-stocked bar. He grabbed a bathrobe and slippers, settling down for a cheerful visit with everyone.

After a reasonable time he announced that we would have to leave in fifteen min-

utes, as we were due for dinner and he had promised his hostess we would not be late. General laughter followed this instruction, but when ten minutes had passed he arose, opened the front door, and with a sweep of his arm bid everyone good night. When the room cleared, he disappeared into the bedroom and reappeared quickly, wearing a neatly pressed blue suit, a pale blue shirt with maroon tie, and a white handkerchief folded into his breast pocket. In his jacket lapel was the rosette of the Legion d'Honneur.

"Just out of curiosity," I asked, "where are we going?"

"To dine with the Yul Brynners. "They live in Switzerland but are in Paris for a few days, and this was the only time we could get together. I hope you don't mind."

"Not at all," I replied. "Yul and I once worked together many years ago. Do they know you're bringing a friend?"

"Of course," he answered. "He's looking forward to seeing you again."

We went off to a small, three-star restaurant tucked into a tiny side street. In front of the building, jammed against the opposite wall with its wheels extended into the roadway, was the largest chic-bloated Rolls-Royce I'd ever seen. It hogged the block and prevented traffic from entering or leaving the narrow alleyway. I noticed it had Swiss license plates and a brown-uniformed chauffeur sitting in front, smoking a cigarette, and reading a newspaper. It impressed me as more than a bit ostentatious.

As we entered the dining room, Yul Brynner got up to greet Isaac. He looked at me with no recognition, and Isaac filled the void by introducing me as his recording

ISAAC STERN

New York City
March 3, 1992

Surely Isaac Stern must have swallowed a Stradivarius, so eloquent are his words. Ask him to expound on music, on virtuosity, on performing, and you'll come away with "Isaacisms." I chose to concentrate on Stern's face rather than on the stereotype image of violinist with violin. But when he went to a drawer to locate a bow, it was a fresh angle of master and instrument, and evoked his own words: "There has to be a feeling as if the instrument is something that's part of you—that you want to enfold the instrument . . . that it's something that is a loved, desired object."

—J.D.R.

"boss." Brynner nodded and waved vaguely in the direction of his wife, who, extending a warm smile and handshake, indicated I should sit next to her. She was an extraordinarily beautiful woman; as dinner progressed I found she was also charming and bright.

At the end of the meal Brynner finally said to me: "I seem to know you. Why?"

I started to answer but his interest had faded; his wife squeezed my hand.

When we left the restaurant the Rolls-Royce was still there and, much to my surprise, as soon as we appeared the chauffeur leapt out and opened the nearest door. The Brynners said their good-byes and entered the car, waving to us as the door closed. Isaac and I watched in amusement as the vehicle carefully eased into the narrow street and pulled away with the unmistakable sound of expensive automobile engineering.

Isaac and I worked closely on a number of major recording projects. These included, in addition to concerti and recital disks, the formation of the Stern-Istomin-Rose Trio.

Not since 1905, when Casals joined forces with the pianist Alfred Cortot and the violinist Jacques Thibaud, had any three major musicians devoted a substantial part of their yearly activities to playing this exquisite repertoire. The Casals-Cortot-Thibaud Trio did this for about a month each year, except during the years of the First World War, until well into the 1930s, and their example of collegial artistry had always been in the back of Isaac's mind. In 1961 he asked his friends Eugene Istomin and the cellist Leonard Rose to join him in some experimental concerts, and after the three felt artistically comfortable with each other, he approached me with the idea of making some records. I hesitated at first, knowing historically this was a difficult repertoire to sell, but his impassioned and committed belief won me over. We began a project that, much to my pleasant surprise, coincided with the listening public's newfound fascination with chamber repertoire. The records sold well, but our continuing plans were brought to an end by the premature death of Leonard Rose.

After Rose's death, Isaac undertook recording the ten Beethoven violin sonatas with Istomin. Some of these he had recorded earlier with Zakin; as an artist he now wanted to reexamine this major repertoire.

An *artist:* what does that word really mean? In this careless world of ours it is bandied about with abandon, often applied to the most patent nonsense, whether visual, literary, or performed. In more leisurely and perhaps better ordered moments in human affairs, artist was a word used with great care to denote someone whose talents had been sharpened by continuing experience and age, and in the case of a musician, someone whose intellect and curiosity had led him or her to reexamine familiar repertoire and explore it for new sounds and ideas. Isaac Stern is a deeply committed artist in the full sense of that honorable and important word. His mind is a searching one, his intellectual capacity boundless, and I believe much of this strength is nurtured by his relationship with his family—his wife, Vera; his daughter, Shira, a rabbi; his two musician sons, Michael and David; and his grandchildren.

There is little difference between Stern the traveling artist and Stern the husband and father. If a yearlong tour became too hectic, there was always time put aside for an off-season trip involving everyone. Once, in 1962, such a trip brought the Stern family to Cape Cod, near our summer home.

On the Labor Day weekend that year, we were in the throes of closing up our house. On Saturday night our telephone rang about 9:00 P.M. The Sterns had been caught in bad traffic and were further delayed by an accident that clogged the highway. They were in need of a place to spend the night; could we take them in? Our children were already in bed and the larder was practically empty, but we gave them directions and in short order heard their car in the driveway. As they emerged they were obviously travel strained after hours of fighting traffic in the late summer heat. We suggested a swim and explained that we had very little food in the house but would find something.

Within minutes, beds had been made up and sandwiches improvised. The Stern kids, having cooled off with a dip, were seated at our dining table, full of smiles. When their meager supper was presented, they wolfed everything in sight and afterward piled into bed and were asleep in minutes. The grown-ups spent a delightful hour or two in conversation and then also headed off for sleep.

The next morning we told our boys about our unexpected visitors, and when the

Stern family emerged, a breakfast of sorts was created out of whatever was left in the kitchen. Isaac immediately had our boys deep in conversation. On being told we had a tennis court nearby, he suggested family tennis, and off he and I trooped with all the children clutching rackets and an odd collection of tennis balls.

I had, of course, completely forgotten that Isaac, born in Russia, had left that country as a baby and been brought up in California, a state synonymous with tennis. Looking at him physically, then and now, you would not suppose he was athletic. He's not very tall and, apart from sinewy arms and muscular hands, is generally round. Looking at him across a tennis net is an odd sensation—you can barely see the top of his head. We divided by families; Isaac and Michael were to take on me and my son Henry.

As soon as we started volleying, I knew the Chapin side was in deep trouble. Michael's returns were straight and powerful for a boy; Isaac's were deadly field artillery.

We had a wonderful fathers-and-sons morning; the fact that we were beaten 6–0 did not dampen our enthusiasm. After we'd finished our formal set, Isaac asked the other boys onto the court, and for the rest of the morning gave tennis lessons. By noontime everyone was ready for a swim, and like the Pied Piper, Isaac had all the children following him into the water. Our boys were strong swimmers, and it wasn't long before they were showing the Stern children some aquatic tricks.

After the Sterns resumed their journey, I realized that not for a single moment had any of us had the feeling that we were dealing with a "star." We had been joined by a gregarious, energetic, and caring family, rather like our own, and the fact that the father was a world celebrity meant nothing whatever. He was not subtly demanding, as is often the case with prominent people who masquerade egos behind a seeming interest in others; he was the paterfamilias in the full sense of the word. He gains extraordinary strength from that role, strength that continually fuels his talents and has kept him, for almost fifty-six years, one of the world's musical superstars.

André Previn

first met André Previn in 1960, while I was director of Masterworks for Columbia Records (now Sony Classical). A colleague of mine, Irving Townsend, wanted to sign a contract with Previn for a series of pop and jazz albums; André insisted he wanted to record at least one classical piano or chamber music album a year as well, and would not agree to any of Columbia's terms without that specific provision.

Townsend came to my office to discuss this request, thinking, I suppose, that I was too head-in-the-clouds to have heard of Previn. I leapt at the opportunity to work with one of the finest musical talents of our time, a man whose skills as a composer and pianist in film and jazz I knew well, but whose sharpest gifts as a conductor I was soon to help uncover. During that journey of discovery our professional association developed into a lasting friendship.

At Columbia, my initial commitment to André was for one record of piano pieces a year, and while this seemed simple enough I had to point out that I needed to be extremely careful about repertoire. We already had a number of world-class pianists under exclusive contract, including Rudolf Serkin, Glenn Gould, Gary Graffman, Eugene Istomin, Alexander Brailowsky, Clara Haskill, and Robert Casadesus (Goddard Lieberson, the president of the company, and I were also involved in secret negotiations with Vladimir Horowitz). André understood, making it clear he was prepared to look at Hindemith, Poulenc, Roussel, and other moderns instead of the classics. I liked his professionalism and especially his subtle humor, which aided and abetted our discussion.

That afternoon we settled on his first recording, a pairing of Hindemith's piano Sonata No. 3 with Samuel Barber's *Four Excursions* and the Prelude No. 7 of Frank Martin. This was hardly repertoire to race up the popularity charts, but the choices demonstrated his eclectic tastes and virtuosic skills while at the same time filling a Columbia catalog need. We agreed to meet in California early in 1961 to consider some chamber recordings with the old Roth String Quartet, the group with which he made his first serious music recordings as a very young man in the 1940s.

Over the next months I didn't see much of Previn but we'd talk on the phone a fair amount, planning projects that included recording Shostakovich's first piano concerto with Bernstein and the New York Philharmonic and his arranging and conducting an album of popular standards for Eileen Farrell. Farrell had just had an enormous success with her first pop album *I've Got a Right to Sing the Blues,* and Irving Townsend suggested that André's song arrangements might be just the right follow-up. Farrell herself was enthusiastic, and I went with her to Hollywood for the sessions. It was on this trip I realized that Previn, for all his talent and skill in a wide variety of musical endeavors, was really born to be a conductor.

This feeling did not spring from the Farrell sessions (although these were impressive in their own right), but developed over the few days I spent with him while he was scoring a movie at the Warner Brothers studio and conducting an ad hoc orchestra made up of studio musicians who played symphonic music for their own pleasure.

At the studio he had a large ensemble that had to rehearse and record a new score (his own) in precious little time. He wasted none of it. On the podium he was concise, giving his explanations in understandable language overlaced with occasional gentle humor. I could see the musicians straighten up and lean forward to hear what he had to say. When he actually started conducting, his beat was clear, his gestures precise; he was at one with the players.

A day later I again watched him with the ad hoc group. There was an unmistakable aura of authority and professionalism about him. I began to feel certain that with time and experience he could become a classical conductor of the first rank. The question was whether or not this idea interested him.

Following the ad hoc rehearsals, Dory, André, and I dined at the Scandia restaurant in Hollywood. Over dinner I asked what he really wanted to do with his life. The two of them exchanged knowing glances; obviously this was a subject they'd discussed before. "More than anything in the world, I want to conduct," he said finally, holding Dory's hand. "That's been my ambition for years. That's what I *really* want to do!"

Now, I was already aware of his success on the pop-concert circuit, conducting assorted light repertoire and playing the piano in programs that inevitably included either the Gershwin Concerto in F or *Rhapsody in Blue.* I asked if any of the orchestras he visited ever offered him an engagement as a guest conductor. The answer was no except for one: the St. Louis Symphony. Because of his pop-concert success in that city the orchestra, under the prodding of its imaginative manager, William "Willy" Zalken, had invited him for three years in a row to conduct subscription concerts in their regular winter season. Further, Zalken allowed him to program whatever he liked. He was scheduled to conduct there again in early 1962.

The next morning I called my friend Willy Zalken, whose opinions about André's talents were even more emphatic than mine. Willy was not only manager of the St. Louis Symphony, he also ran the St. Louis Municipal Opera, where he staged musical theater, operettas, and pops concerts. He'd spotted André's talent the first time he appeared. I reminded Willy of an old Columbia contract with the St. Louis Symphony that technically had one more recording to be completed, and wondered if he'd like to take a chance with me on André's first symphonic disk. He agreed immediately.

With this commitment I went to hear André's first 1962 St. Louis subscription

concert without telling him I had a recording project in mind. I wanted to see how he actually behaved on the podium in front of a full-fledged symphony orchestra. What I saw in one two-and-a-half-hour rehearsal and subsequent performances convinced me I was right: here was a major talent for whom little yet had been possible in the classical orchestral field. He would obviously have a hard time overcoming his Hollywood background, but if this was what he really wanted to do I was confident of his immense talent and felt the best introduction might be the unexpected symphonic recording.

After his concert we had supper together. I was looking into the face of a happy man, not smugly satisfied with his concert—about which he had a few acid observations to make on what he perceived to be his own inadequacies and inexperience—but happy in the broad sense of having found inner peace. It was obvious he really wanted the symphonic world to be his artistic home. Taking a breath, I then suggested the recording, explaining my odd situation with the St. Louis Symphony. His smile could have illuminated the entire city.

As with his piano disks, I could not offer him the Mozart, Brahms, Beethoven, or Tchaikovsky repertoire that might receive broad notice, since we had Bruno Walter, Igor Stravinsky, Leonard Bernstein, Eugene Ormandy, and George Szell under exclusive contracts, but the choice of material turned out to be surprisingly easy.

At an earlier concert in St. Louis he had conducted Benjamin Britten's *Symphonia da Requiem,* an excellent and deeply moving composition from 1941. The music was of great interest to André, and what appealed to me was the fact that the only previous recording was one conducted by the composer in monophonic sound. We then talked back and forth about the other side of the disk, finally settling on Aaron Copland's orchestral suite from his film score for *The Red Pony.* I think we were both a little worried whether the Britten/Copland coupling would work. It did.

From the critics the immediate reaction was surprise. Most of the music world had no inkling that André had designs on a conducting career outside the world of movie scoring; virtually none were prepared for the thoughtful, credible readings he gave to the *Symphonia da Requiem* and *The Red Pony* score. Even with an orchestra like St. Louis, at that point taxed to the limit of its skills, André's energy, understanding, and firm hand all came through on the recording. Despite the predictable murmurings of it's being too Hollywoody—the ready rationale stemming from the Copland work's film genesis—a thrill of promise shot through the classical music world.

The release of the *Red Pony* record, as it has come to be called by followers of André's career, was unquestionably the breakthrough he needed. The next step was a manager.

I was surprised to find that up until this point in his life he'd sorted out his own work schedule. Conducting was going to be different: if he was to succeed, he would need someone to look after his interests, to find, select, and secure for him the right opportunities with the right orchestras.

Nor did André have time to waste on mistakes. At age thirty-four he was a little old to be "starting out" as a conductor. Someone who knew the business would have to step in quickly and take advantage of his career's gathering momentum or the parade might quickly pass him by, leaving him only the miasma of Hollywood. Willy Zalken and I talked about these problems and needs and, as it turned out, each, separately and unknown to the other, contacted Ronald Wilford, then—and now—the most powerful and effective manager of conductors in the classical music world.

When I reached Wilford, Zalken's comments had already piqued his interest; my telephone call was the extra push that resulted in a lunch meeting between André, Dory, Wilford, and myself.

At that lunch, held in the Edwardian Room of New York's Plaza hotel, Wilford made clear his interest and conditions. He spoke quietly but with great intensity, and as I looked at André I realized that under his usual cool, almost detached veneer, he was scared stiff. Wilford told him it would be rough—that if he really wanted to conduct he would have to give up Hollywood altogether, except for one picture a year to pay his bills, and that only until his new career caught on. In return he would book him with all kinds of orchestras in order for him to learn both repertoire and how to shape performances with less-than-first-class players. "Conducting is not something you do on the side," Wilford

said. "You do it all the way or not at all. If you're really serious, I propose we work together for a year and at the end of that time decide whether the enterprise is worth continuing." André and Dory exchanged glances. "Let me think about what you've said," he finally told Wilford. "May I let you know later?" Wilford smiled his agreement.

For a few weeks André agonized. He would make great plans one day and abandon them the next; he would weigh heavily the pros and cons, alone on the freeway or in conversations with Dory that often ran through the night. Ultimately, he says, it was an incident straight out of an absurdist drama that shocked him into a decision.

ANDRÉ PREVIN

Bedford Hills, New York
December 18, 1991

Previn was preparing a new song cycle commissioned by Carnegie Hall titled *Honey and Rue*. Submerged in his work, he was oblivious to everything save his music.
—J.D.R.

He was about to score a new film for Twentieth Century–Fox, dealing with a producer whose misunderstandings about music were deep and chronic. After many hours of conversation, the producer told André he'd like to see his ideas on paper. Accustomed to meek compliance with the whims of producers, André went home and turned out a five-page typed proposal for dealing with what he felt were the film's musical requirements.

As he later told his biographers, Martin Bookspan and Ross Yockey, he walked into the producer's office the next morning and handed him the memo. The producer said—and André reported that these were his exact words—"Stick around, kid, while I read this over." André stuck around and watched as the great man in a great studio, sitting behind a desk on which the Ice Follies could have been staged, began reading the memo, moving his lips as he read. "It probably sounds like a small quibble," André commented,

> but all at once it came to me that I was desperately unhappy, working on music I didn't believe in, trying to impress my musical values on a man who moves his lips when he reads. "Excuse me," I said as I rose to my feet.

"You aren't going to understand this, I know, but I've decided I'm not going to do your film." "What the devil are you talking about?" the producer demanded, and I said, "Well, we really haven't signed anything yet, and although you've been very nice, I'm just not going to do it." And so I walked out, fully intending never to set foot in a film studio again.

On his way out, André looked at a clock and saw he still had time to drive home and call New York before the end of the business day there. He told Dory he'd made up his mind. He phoned Ronald Wilford and said he accepted his offer and the conditions.

Wilford was as good as his word. He booked André with great success by taking advantage of his drawing power as a film jazz personality and using his talents as a classical pianist. Sometimes André would play a Mozart or Mendelssohn concerto, conducting from the keyboard. He was allowed to choose the balance of the program. He got an occasional reputable orchestra by filling in at the last minute when a conductor became sick. And he was undergoing the best training imaginable. A great orchestra plays well; the kind that André was conducting needed to be told how to play—to be taught the music—and André had to have strong ideas about what he wanted from them.

Gradually bits and pieces came together. Orchestra managers liked him because he was an economic rehearsal conductor, never wasting time. Audiences responded to his firm musicianship and his obvious joy in and commitment to what he was doing. At the end of that year Wilford agreed to manage him and within a few months arranged for his first orchestral post, as music director of the Houston Symphony. He was on his way.

Today he is one of the most in-demand conductors of our time. Wilford still manages him, his career spans the globe, and as he steps onto podiums wherever they are, his pleasure in being there is contagious. I'm delighted to have had a role in helping start his conducting career, a career that continues to bring extraordinary pleasure to music lovers all over the world.

Jerome Robbins

Since bursting on the scene in the midforties, first as a dancer, then as dancer/choreographer, and now, as age and injuries preclude his being onstage, as choreographer and stage director, Jerome Robbins continues to be a seminal influence on American dance. Together with the late Agnes de Mille, he led the breakthrough from kick chorus to choreographed storytelling in Broadway musicals.

In the early 1950s it was Robbins's idea to place the Romeo and Juliet story in a modern urban setting. The result was *West Side Story.* Before that, in his first collaboration with Leonard Bernstein, he created *Fancy Free,* a ballet about three wartime sailors on a one-day leave in New York City. The success of that venture led to the expansion of the ballet into *On the Town,* a full-scale musical which not only launched Bernstein and Robbins as major forces in the musical theater, but launched Betty Comden and Adolph Green as well. Betty and Adolph wrote the show's book and lyrics and played two of the leading characters. For all of these four collaborators, *On the Town* was their first big popular success. Since then Robbins has moved between musical theater and formal dance, creating a memorable body of work in both disciplines.

My association with him began socially, in the early sixties, when we were introduced by Leonard Bernstein. Shortly thereafter he and I had our first professional negotiations concerning a summertime revival of *West Side Story* at Lincoln Center. I soon discovered that his enormous creative talents were matched by a fierce drive to protect what he perceived to be his own business interests. In short order I found myself completely trapped between a rock and a very hard place, he making it quite clear that for a variety of personal reasons the revival would not take place. It took Stephen Sondheim's low-key intervention to finally bring our talks to a successful conclusion.

The next time we met I was working as Leonard Bernstein's executive producer. We discussed his wish to have Bernstein as pianist and conductor for his staging of Stravinsky's ballet *Les Noces* for the New York City Ballet. This time his attitude was different: he was a model of courtesy and understanding. I soon realized that in those talks he wanted something from me.

In any event, watching this man work with the *Les Noces* dancers was like watching a marine drill sergeant in full cry: he had everyone's attention, probably out of equal parts love and fear. When he called a break, the company collapsed as one, sliding to the floor in a state of absolute exhaustion. The break ended with Robbins clapping his hands, immediately causing me to abandon the drill-sergeant simile in favor of likening him to General Patton. Whatever Robbins did, though, and however he did it, the talent and discipline worked. *Les Noces* was a critical and public triumph.

Shortly after *Les Noces,* it was again my turn to want something from Robbins. After Goeran Gentele's death I asked if he would consider directing Gentele's *Carmen* production as a memorial to a man whom I knew he admired.

On July 19, 1972, I reached him at Saratoga Springs, New York, where he was overseeing the New York City Ballet at their summer quarters. He immediately agreed to have a look at the production models but was not encouraging about his participation.

When he arrived at my office he looked at everything with a painstaking eye. "You have nothing to worry about," he said. "The production is already a success." He

JEROME ROBBINS

New York City
April 22, 1992

To quote Sondheim's concise observation on Jerome Robbins: **"Paradoxes make him." I'd heard stories of Robbins's growl; I perceived—paradoxically—a gentle nature . . . albeit a somewhat impatient one. His impatience in front of the camera—again paradoxically—only masked a shyness at being photographed: "Lenny was comfortable with this sort of thing. I'm afraid I don't make a very good subject." Soon a frisky dog vaguely resembling a golden retriever bounded into the room, intent on taking center stage. The dog was a pale buff color, with one eye dark brown, the other ice blue. I learned her name was Tess—that Jerry had found her on the steps of the Metropolitan Museum of Art one afternoon. She had had no collar or identification tags, and followed him home as if glued to his leg. He took the usual measures— phoning vets, posting notices—but no one claimed the dog. Tess, instead, claimed Jerry.   —J.D.R.**

elaborated his view that the whole concept and physical realization of it were daring and brilliant and that, because of Gentele's tragic death and the public sympathy for this colorful and engaging man, almost anyone could follow through. "What about you?" I asked. "No, Schuyler, I cannot, much as I would like to help you. I'm simply not physically up to it, and if I ever did an opera I would want to start from scratch. Later we might talk about *Salome.* I've some thoughts about this curious piece." And he arose to go. "But remember what I've said," he murmured quietly as we shook hands, "*Carmen* is already a success." Later he wrote me an affectionate letter expressing the same thoughts. During my years at the Met I'm only sorry we never got around to pursuing *Salome.*

Jerome Robbins continues to astound. Recently *Jerome Robbins' Broadway,* a collection of dances from his various musicals, played at the Imperial Theater. The first act closed with a suite of his incredible dances from *West Side Story.*

As I went outside for the intermission, I ran into Walter and Jean Kerr. The three of us had tears in our eyes. "God, what talent," Jean said. Walter and I looked at each other and nodded in full agreement.

There is only one Robbins. He is still quite impossible to deal with, but most of us can forgive his quirks when the beauty, sensitivity, and vitality of his work is on the stage for the world to share.

Stephen Sondheim

My first meeting with Stephen Sondheim took place on a hot July morning in 1962, the year of *A Funny Thing Happened on the Way to the Forum,* his first Broadway show as both composer and lyricist. Earlier, he'd collaborated with Leonard Bernstein on *West Side Story* and Jule Styne on *Gypsy,* and would soon collaborate with Richard Rodgers on *Do I Hear a Waltz?,* but with *Forum* he was beginning to charge off on his own.

That day I was waiting in a stifling terminal at New York's La Guardia airport to board a plane for Martha's Vineyard. Tucked into my hand luggage was a test pressing of *On the Town,* Bernstein's own recording of his first musical. As the director of Columbia Masterworks, I needed his approval before publicly releasing the recording, and since the Bernsteins were summering on the Vineyard, they invited me to spend a couple of days there while the maestro made his decisions.

As I glanced around the fetid room, my eyes lit on what looked like a young derelict, curled up in a broken chair, sound asleep in a cramped, almost fetal position. He badly needed a shave and haircut and his clothes looked as if they'd been on him for weeks. I remember a stab of sorrow, wondering what on earth had brought this unknown man to such a sorry state of disarray.

Presently my flight was called. I was surprised to see the fellow untangle himself and shuffle toward the same plane, where he boarded just ahead of me, immediately collapsing into a seat and asleep before the rest of us had settled in.

During the flight I read a magazine and dozed a bit, but from time to time I couldn't help glancing across the aisle, where, as sunlight occasionally streamed across his face, the derelict looked pale and exhausted. He was still asleep when we began landing procedures. I noticed the stewardess, with some caution, lean over to check that his seat belt was properly fastened.

When we touched down, the plane taxied to a small airport terminal and I saw the young man drag himself slowly to his feet, rubbing his eyes and yawning. He slipped behind me as we moved toward the exit.

As I stepped off the plane, Leonard and Felicia Bernstein were waving cheerfully at me, but when they spotted the untidy fellow just behind my head, they both rushed forward to embrace him. I was a touch puzzled. My greeting was hospitable enough but his was overwhelming. In an instant the three had their arms around each other.

"Have you met Steve Sondheim?" Lenny asked. The four of us walked toward the baggage area while my mind reeled. *That* bag of rags is Steve Sondheim?

En route to the Bernstein house, it wasn't long before I found that while working together both men had discovered a mutual passion for the crazed world of word games and puzzles. I quickly realized my recording approvals would have to be sandwiched between assembling jigsaw puzzles and solving English newspaper crosswords.

That first day I enjoyed Felicia's company until the evening, when the household all came together for dinner. Around the dinner table I learned the two friends also shared another bond: both were night people, rarely going to bed until the early morning hours. Sondheim had obviously not been to bed at all on the night before our flight.

I cannot say Steve and I became bosom buddies during that long weekend, but over the subsequent thirty-odd years we have developed a comfortable friendship. He realizes I'm not an unsuccessful facilitator; I know that this bright, scruffy, talented fellow has, in a word, revolutionized the American musical.

STEPHEN SONDHEIM

*New York City
May 28, 1992*

Sondheim was in a dark mood, and having his picture taken was not one of his pleasures—a task he has always dreaded. "I never know what to do in front of a camera," he confessed. With empathy I assured him it would be a painless procedure, that he wouldn't have to "do" anything but just "be." "I'll do the seeing," I said. I arranged pose and composition, lit Sondheim accordingly, looked through the lens, and told him, "Now you're just going to think. *Just think.*" I began shooting, the rhythmic click of the shutter the only sound. He was relaxed, oblivious of the camera—lost in thought. For a moment his brow furrowed, only to soften. What cloud, I wondered, had passed across his mind? —**J.D.R.**

Stephen Sondheim was born on March 22, 1930. A precocious child, he skipped kindergarten, read *The New York Times* in the first grade, and even had the sense to be self-conscious about being the smartest kid in his class. "I would purposely drop my *g*'s," he told his biographer, Craig Zadan, "because I spoke English so well."

At the age of ten, Sondheim's essentially quiet childhood underwent a sharp upheaval when his parents were divorced. His mother moved to a farm in Doylestown, Pennsylvania, and that move had a lot to do with his initial interest in the musical theater. "Among my mother's acquaintances in Pennsylvania was the Oscar Hammerstein family," he told Zadan. "They had a son, Jimmy, who was my age, and we became close friends very quickly. Since the Hammersteins lived only three miles from us, they gradually became surrogate parents for me."

Around that time, Hammerstein was working on a new musical called *Oklahoma!* and before long, with Hammerstein's "nudging," adolescent Sondheim became intrigued with the musical theater. At the age of fifteen, he and two classmates wrote a musical about their campus life called *By George,* in honor of the Quaker-run George School in Bucks County, Pennsylvania, which all three were attending. "I really thought it was terrific," Sondheim remembers.

And when I finished it, I not only wanted Oscar to see it, but I wanted him to be the first to read it, because I just knew he and Dick Rodgers would want to produce it immediately and I'd be the first fifteen-year-old ever to have a musical done on Broadway.

So I gave it to him one evening and told him to read it objectively, as though he didn't know me, as something that crossed his desk on a totally professional level. And I went home that night with delusions of grandeur in my head. I could see my name in lights. Next day when I got up he called and I went over to his house, and he said, "Now you want my opinion as though I really didn't know you? Well, it's the worst thing I've ever read." And he probably saw that my lower lip began to tremble, and he said, "Now I didn't say it was untalented, I said it was terrible. And if you want to know *why* it's terrible, I'll tell you."

Hammerstein proceeded from the very first stage direction to go through every song, scene, and line of dialogue. "At the risk of hyperbole," Sondheim recalls,

I'd say that in that afternoon I learned more about songwriting and the musical theater than most people learn in a lifetime. I was getting the distillation of thirty years of experience. And he did indeed treat me as if I was a professional.

Hammerstein's comments made a deep impression on the youngster, but it wasn't until he went to Williams College, where in his freshman year he took an elective course in music, that his career pattern began to be shaped. Sondheim told Zadan: "The teacher, Robert Barrow, was so sensational that if he'd taught geology I would probably have become a geologist. Before Barrow I waited for all the tunes to come into my head. I was a romantic. He taught me to first learn the technique and then put the notes down on paper . . . that's what music is." Upon graduation, Sondheim won the Hutchinson Prize, a two-year fellowship which he utilized to study with the avant-garde composer Milton Babbitt.

Babbitt, an old friend and colleague of mine from the Columbia-Princeton Electronic Music Center, had this to say about his outstanding pupil:

> I was teaching at Princeton and tutored very few students individually. In fact, Steve was the last person I taught privately. He had good basic training in music at Williams, a great deal of music intelligence, and through a certain amount of listening to records and piano playing, he had quite a broad background. He made it clear immediately that he wasn't interested in becoming what one would call a serious composer, but he wanted to know a great deal about so-called serious music because he thought it would be suggestive and useful.
>
> Steve came as a sort of Ivy League young man who had decided to go into music after having thought about other alternatives. He learned very quickly. He had a very nimble mind and he was very musical. He worked slowly, even on what might seem to be simple material. He claimed that he was lazy, but I think it takes him a long time to satisfy himself.

Babbitt's last observation was right on the money: I began finding this out when I became involved in the recording plans for *Anyone Can Whistle,* Sondheim's 1964 show that lasted on Broadway for all of nine performances.

The show itself, about conformity, nonconformity, idealism, and romanticism in contemporary society, has become a favorite cult musical. The book was ponderous but it had one of Sondheim's most inventive scores. The show has never been revived on Broadway, but the score, with its brilliant music and complex lyrics sung by the show's original cast—Lee Remick, Angela Lansbury, and Harry Guardino—is still around because of a decision made by Goddard Lieberson, then the president of Columbia

Records, to record the show even though not contractually bound to do so unless it had run for twenty-one performances. Lieberson consulted me about the decision and I agreed wholeheartedly, particularly as we both realized we wanted to invest in Sondheim's talent, not in the success or lack of success of one particular show. Steve never forgot this faith on the part of Columbia Records: subsequent shows were always offered first to the label. The show itself was dedicated to Goddard Lieberson.

Shortly after *Whistle,* I left Columbia to become program chief for Lincoln Center, and that year the Musical Theater of Lincoln Center, under the artistic direction of Richard Rodgers, wanted to produce a summertime revival of *West Side Story.* The creative partners were at odds about this idea: Bernstein, the composer, and Arthur Laurents, author of the book, agreed to the project, but Jerome Robbins emphatically did not, refusing to give his permission. I was desperate; there was no logical reason for his stubbornness, but the more he was asked, the more he dug in his heels. Bernstein couldn't budge him, neither could Laurents, so one day I called Sondheim, who as lyricist of this his first show had not yet voiced an opinion. I asked if he'd join me in one more attempt to get Robbins to change his mind. He agreed. A day later the three of us met in Robbins's house.

After I'd made a presentation of the production plans, Steve was eloquent in defending my position. I saw a look of surprise spread across Robbins's face—perhaps he'd assumed Steve would automatically support his views—and soon, much to my amazement, the argument ended in favor of our moving ahead. Steve smiled shyly at me as I hastily withdrew before Robbins could change his mind. As it happened this revival was a tremendous success. Steve had played a pivotal role in making it all happen.

Over the years, Sondheim's talents were sharpened by his long-time association with producer/director Harold Prince. Both men, perhaps without realizing it, were moving the American musical more in the direction of grand opera than the traditional Broadway show. Steve often bristled when I'd discuss this point with him, particularly after I became general manager of the Metropolitan and tried to persuade him to consider a commission from us, but bristle or not, successive shows became more operatic. *Pacific Overtures* was one of these, *A Little Night Music* certainly was operetta at its most seductive, and with *Sweeney Todd* he wrote a full-blown modern opera, even if he hated hearing the show defined as such.

During that show's opening night I was accosted by Harold Clurman, then dean of New York theater critics. Clurman demanded to know why *Sweeney Todd* was not on the stage of the Metropolitan. "Did you try to get it?" he bellowed, in his husky authoritative voice. I told him that if I'd had my way I would have wanted the honor of its world premiere. Clurman sniffed in a way that could be interpreted as satisfaction with my answer.

Shortly before *Sweeney Todd* opened, the American soprano Evelyn Lear presented a lieder recital at New York's Town Hall. In preparing for this event she decided to include a group of Sondheim songs. Steve called me in something of a panic because he had the firmly fixed idea that opera and concert singers did not understand his material. I told him Evelyn Lear was a first-rate artist who specialized in modern repertoire, as well as being a brilliant opera singer/actor who would respond well to his coaching. They met, and while working together she persuaded Steve to let her add the unheard *Sweeney Todd* aria "Green Finch and Linnet Bird" to her program, an aria whose decidedly Schubertian line fit perfectly between the songs of Wolf and Poulenc.

My wife and I caught Steve sneaking into Town Hall the afternoon of her recital. I know he was totally unprepared for the ovation that cascaded around him when Lear completed his cycle. Blushing furiously, he had to rise several times and acknowledge the applause before the audience calmed down enough to allow the concert to continue.

Over the past few years, my personal association with Sondheim has been reinforced by my son, Ted, the president and executive director of the Rodgers and Hammerstein Organization and overseer of the Irving Berlin catalogs. It was Ted who sparked the idea of uniting the Sondheim forces with the New York Philharmonic to present the now-famous concerts and recording of *Follies*. Those performances, together with the television documentary made about them, serve to remind the public what monumental talent continues to pour out from the pen of this unique artist, working slowly and painfully, as he does, over every note and every word.

Stephen Sondheim often pays a price for his talent. He's extremely critical of people and situations around him, sometimes frighteningly so, but he's hardest of all on himself. Over the years I've realized that even though he's a very sophisticated musician, that sophistication often gets in the way of a simple emotional statement. As he grows older, I'm happy to say that in my view his work is becoming more direct, though he never lets go of his vulnerability.

I once heard Sondheim, seated at a small grand piano on the stage of the Shubert Theater in New York, sing the title song from *Anyone Can Whistle*. As I listened, it suddenly struck me that what I was actually hearing was the simple, vivid description of Sondheim the man and artist himself:

Anyone can whistle,
That's what they say—
       Easy.
Anyone can whistle
Any old day—
       Easy.
It's all so simple:
Relax, let go, let fly.
So someone tell me why
       Can't I?
I can dance a tango,
I can read Greek—
       Easy.
I can slay a dragon
Any old week—
       Easy.
What's hard is simple,
What's natural comes hard.
Maybe you could show me
       How to let go
       Lower my guard,
       Learn to be free.
Maybe if you whistle,
       Whistle for me.

Sir Peter Ustinov

ctor, writer, novelist, dramatist, wit, mimic, raconteur, humorist, director, producer, goodwill ambassador, cartoonist, and, above all, humanitarian: Peter Ustinov's gifts—I should say *Sir* Peter Ustinov's gifts; he was knighted in 1990—and accomplishments are almost too many and too diverse to enumerate. What is occasionally left out of any list, however, is his absolute passion for music, which in one way or another has played a major role in his life—all kinds of music, from Josquin to Schnittke, including both composers and performers. He imitates whole orchestras, assorted horn players, violinists, cellists, tympanists, operatic ensembles, singers, conductors, pianists, organists, critics, and musicologists, all the while not being able to read a single note himself. I remember once in the 1960s, as we were sitting together at a New York Philharmonic spring Promenade Concert about to hear a piece by the contemporary Swiss composer Frank Martin, I confessed that Martin was one of the few Swiss composers I'd ever heard of and thought perhaps there weren't many others in that land of finance, munitions, and cuckoo clocks.

He looked at me tolerantly, and as the houselights dimmed reached for his pen. The next thing I knew he handed me a list of at least forty names crammed all over both sides of a tiny scrap of paper he'd conveniently found in his pocket. I later checked through *Groves Dictionary of Music and Musicians* and found every one of them listed.

But as Christopher Warwick, author of the charming biography *The Universal Ustinov,* points out, who or what is the *essential* Peter Ustinov? "The man is so amazingly complex," said the actor Paul Rogers to Warwick, "that it would amount to impudence even to attempt to discover that."

Today Ustinov's admirers include all sorts of world leaders and statesmen, kings and princes, members of the international business community, relief agencies, and, not least, people within the various denominations of that global fraternity we refer to as "the arts." Their respect clearly stems from the recognition that he is not only endowed with an especially fine mind—"an intimidating intelligence" as one journalist put it—but that for much of his life he has found himself in the rare position of observing and commenting on a wide range of sociopolitical issues, relevant not just to any one nation, but to the world as a whole.

Peter and I first met on a spring evening in 1958, when the gangling young Van Cliburn, having just become an American hero by winning the Tchaikovsky Piano Competition in Moscow, returned to New York for a ticker-tape parade up lower Broadway, a huge indigestible civic lunch in the grand ballroom of the Waldorf-Astoria Hotel, and a Sunday night prime-time television appearance playing the last movement of Tchaikovsky's B-flat Minor Concerto. My wife and I were guests at a small post-television party given by our friend Skitch Henderson, the conductor for the occasion, and Skitch's wife, Ruth, at their apartment just off New York City's Gramercy Park. Curled up in a corner on one of the Hendersons' casual sofas watching the proceedings with affectionate curiosity was a vaguely Falstaffian man sporting an oddly trimmed beard and mustache. For a moment I couldn't place him until he turned and I suddenly recognized Peter Ustinov, then starring in his own play, *Romanoff and Juliet,* on Broadway. Our host brought us over to meet him, introducing my wife as "the former Miss Steinway" and me as one of the music managers concerned with Cliburn's professional affairs. The three of us sat together, shortly joined by Cliburn himself, who was fidgety, nervous, and exhausted— and obviously wanted to be out of the room and away from people. My wife, recognizing his agitation, took him gently by the arm and led him outside and around the corner to a neighborhood hamburger shop, leaving Peter and myself to talk.

In minutes he had me bowled over as he imitated various nabobs of the classical music world and vocalized a one-man performance of the Tchaikovsky concerto as played on a Bechstein, Blütner, Bösendorfer, and Steinway piano. When the evening was over I hoped I'd made a new friend. I was fortunate; I had.

Our friendship really began a year later, when we worked together on a couple of recordings during my tenure as director of Columbia Masterworks, but it firmed up in 1967 at Lincoln Center's Vivian Beaumont Theater, where in collaboration with Alexander H. Cohen and against the background of the Vietnam War, I helped produce the first performances of what is now widely considered to be his finest theatrical achievement, a tour de force concerning the stupidity and immorality of war called *The Unknown Soldier and His Wife*. Subtitled *Two Acts of War Separated by a Truce for Refreshment*, the play is the story of the eternal draftee who, after centuries of unquestioned obedience, ultimately refuses to die for the sake of an authority that, as one of the play's characters puts it, "has no place . . . in a society advanced enough to destroy itself."

About the *The Unknown Soldier* one critic mused about Ustinov: "an examination of what he has written . . . places him as a fundamental moralist, although he squirms to be recognized as such." "I try not to be a finger wagger," says Ustinov. "I don't think I have any right to be. If I do it, then I try to disguise it as much as possible. And you must make that finger attractive so that people don't notice it wagging. I loathe dogma."

The 1967 performances of *The Unknown Soldier,* finger wagged, as they were, by most of the New York critics, nevertheless found large audiences moved to such pitch that at the end of its Lincoln Center run it was transferred to a commercial theater on Broadway. The next year it was produced in Britain at the Chichester Theatre and in 1973 was chosen to officially open the New London Theatre in Drury Lane. In the late seventies and eighties the show toured throughout Europe and the former Soviet Union, where its message hit home no matter the language or political culture. I was pleased to have had a part in its birthing process.

SIR PETER USTINOV

Chicago, Illinois
May 29, 1992

This sitting turned into a raucous occasion: Sir Peter, amused at my outbursts of excitement as I saw *the* expression to capture, followed with a ripping imitation of me taking the picture, complete with Boston accent. But the best was Ustinov singing—*basso profundo*—essaying Russian opera, building to crescendo, arms flailing; then, with face scrunched, attacking the instruments of the orchestra from timpani to piccolo, with a distinctive sound for each: very Ustinov.   —J.D.R.

One additional pleasure I had from the 1967 Lincoln Center experience was introducing Peter to Rolf Liebermann, who promptly persuaded him to plunge into the world of opera by directing Mozart's *Magic Flute* at the Hamburg State Opera, then his home base. Peter needed no second bidding, for while his musical tastes, as noted, embrace everything, he has always been a Mozart devotee. He says:

People often ask me what other writer has influenced me and I've really got to say that I don't think any have. I was very interested in Chekhov and Gorky and those people, but I don't think they actually influenced what I did. *If* anything has influenced me, it's Mozart, because he has what I call the most profound superficiality. He keeps the surface of the water still, so that you can study the complexity of the rocks beneath; which in itself is a splendid achievement, because there's a case of a man who engages you on one level and makes you think on another. And that, I think, is absolutely right.

Ustinov described his treatment of *The Magic Flute* in these terms: "I made this fictitious Egyptian kingdom on the stage look very much like a university campus . . .

like a cross section of civilization. It attracted severe criticism, especially from traditional-ists. Some time later, when the same production was staged in Florence, however, the *New York Herald Tribune* openly questioned what had displeased German audiences, adding that it was 'surely respectful of the text . . . faithful to the music and yet inventive.'"

I can only say that my wife and I journeyed to Hamburg to see this production and found it refreshing, imaginative, and theatrical, even more fascinating than the Chagall production that was later to grace the stage of the Metropolitan during my tenure as general manager.

Aided by a lifetime of observing humanity in all its manifestations, Peter Ustinov has also earned a well-deserved reputation for being one of the world's foremost racon-teurs. Because of his constant travel, he's in a unique position to add to his repertoire, rotating characters and stories to suit the occasion.

One such opportunity occurred at the meetings of what became known as the UNESCO Roundtable on Arts and Culture in the New World Order, a group of artists, impresarios, and educators organized by Peter, Jean d'Ormesson of the French Academy, the late Hepzibah Menuhin, and the late English philosopher and peace worker Philip Noel-Baker. The delegates were, for the most part, private citizens, invited by the orga-nizers to take part. I was delighted when Ustinov suggested I be one of the American rep-resentatives.

About thirty of us assembled in the famous *salle* 7 at the UNESCO headquarters in Paris. Seated to my left was a shy gentleman from Norway with the unlikely name of Brattoli. When his turn came to speak he began telling his life story, a story punctuated by long episodes of unemployment, breadlines, wartime hardships, postwar unemploy-ment, strikes, lockouts, and other constantly difficult situations. Then, without pausing, he described a horrendous fishing industry crisis during which he lost his job, "after which I became prime minister."

I was sitting opposite Ustinov, whose eyebrows rose at this astonishing statement and stayed in an upright position as Mr. Moutra, the chief delegate from India, brought out a series of photographs demonstrating how his country had solved the world's energy crisis. "Cow dung," he said in sepulchral tones, sending the photographs around the table.

And as if this wasn't enough, there was fellow American delegate Buckminster Fuller, the great inventor and engineer, whose deafness couldn't be overcome because his hearing aid, one he'd invented himself, would only work on special batteries, which he'd also invented but had unfortunately left at home. This meant that Bucky (as he was called by almost everyone) was often unaware of how loud and fast he was talking, creating enormous confusion among the delegates and at one point causing the translators—Chinese, English, German, Italian, Russian—to run out of their second-floor translation booths down to the delegates' floor to plead in person for him to slow down.

Peter took all these incidents (and others!) from the meetings, weaving them into a tapestry of anecdotes that always leaves his listeners hopelessly limp with laughter, not only because the incidents themselves are funny but because he always finds the right way of giving each adventure a warm, compassionate touch. Over the years I keep remembering certain old favorites—the ancient cleric "who spoke as though he had a cathedral in the back of his mouth" or the crusty old Englishman who's been known to put in an "appearance" when life in the United States comes under discussion. He's the type of character who, having been told once too often to "have a nice day," snaps back "I have *other* plans!"

In the autumn of 1979, Ustinov took a bold step in his career as an actor: he decided to make his first foray into Shakespeare, choosing to accept an invitation from the Stratford [Ontario] Festival to play the lead in a new production of *King Lear.*

If, as with his charge into opera, the by-now fifty-eight-year-old seemed kind of old for a first attempt of Shakespeare, his characteristic reply was: "I've got three daughters of my own, which is a more thorough rehearsal for the part than anything Stanislavsky ever suggested."

Directed by Robin Phillips, Ustinov's *Lear* was no distant drama shrouded in ancient shadows. Instead it was set in the 1850s, around the time of the Crimean War. "I think we use that 'ancient Britain' too much when we want to make everything rather remote," Peter said at the time, adding that

Lear is a play that can be adapted to the court life of the last century. It's a military play, a play about hierarchy. It's also a play about protocol, how Lear discovers with immense pain that we're all naked people, just dressed differently. I think Lear's mad in the beginning, not entirely mad, perhaps, but certainly senile. . . . He can't remember things and won't admit that he can't remember until he finally comes face-to-face with himself from the outside, which of course makes him self-pitying.

During the *Lear* run—and one of only three times he has done so in over thirty years—Peter suggested that he'd be delighted, and my wife and I might not be thoroughly disappointed, if we came up to Stratford to have a look for ourselves. We made the trip and both of us sat in the theater stunned by a *Lear* that genuinely moved us. To me the play is more often cerebrally precise than emotionally engaging. Certainly the old king is a pathetic fool, but by the end of the usual production you're sick and tired of the whole bunch. Not this time. Robin Phillips's superb cast and masterly direction gave Peter a chance to do some of the finest work he's ever done in the theater. During the closing scene, when he appeared holding the dead Cordelia in his arms, I would have given almost anything to have had Stratford's Kleenex concession.

When asked if he would like to play more Shakespeare, Peter had an interesting reply.

No. I'm always delighted when people come up to me—and I must say it happens fairly frequently—and say how much pleasure I've given them. I don't think I'd have given them that much pleasure playing Shakespeare. I enjoyed playing King Lear because I've always had a feeling for him, but otherwise, no, I don't think Shakespeare's for me. I can't see myself *pretending* I know what I'm talking about, like so many distinguished English actors. . . . I don't know what the hell they're talking about— and they don't either. Ralph Richardson was an ace at that. He always gave the impression that he'd made a study of the thing and knew it all and was going to interpret for us.

Now in his midseventies, Sir Peter Ustinov shows no signs of slowing down. I was in Paris for his seventieth birthday, a party at UNESCO jam-packed with his international friends and televised worldwide. In 1991 his novel *The Old Man and Mr. Smith,* the story of God and the devil returning to earth to have a look at their handiwork, was well received by the critics and a great success throughout Europe and America, as was his one-man show *An Evening with Peter Ustinov,* which broke all box-office records at London's Theatre Royal Haymarket. The show was equally successful in its subsequent European, Australian, and New Zealand tours, as well as in San Francisco and Chicago in the United States.

Over the years, because of our mutual fascination with the flawed game of politics, Peter and I have established a kind of private communications code: we often talk to each other as if we were two idiotic United States senators. This idiosyncrasy was tolerated by my tolerant wife, but I suspect Helene Ustinov, Peter's wife who brings such happiness to him, thinks us both quite mad.

Helene du Lau d'Allemans, now Lady Ustinov, is a dark-haired, vivacious Parisienne with a husky voice and bubbling sense of humor whom he first met in the early 1950s and then again in the late sixties. From the moment of their second encounter, Peter and Helene became inseparable. In his autobiography *Dear Me,* he wrote of Helene: "She has made me into something approaching the man I once hoped to be, privately and secretly. She came to my rescue at a turning point during that exhausting, terrifying, and magnificent journey of self-discovery we call life. And for that, I am endlessly grateful."

In returning the compliment, Helene told Christopher Warwick: "Peter is really the happiness of my life. He is an exceptional man. A genius. People like him should live eternally."

James Levine

On January 1, 1994, I attended the Met's twenty-fifth performance of Hector Berlioz's gigantic *Les Troyens,* an opera whose first Met production took place in October 1973 during my management, conducted this time by James Levine. Originally conducted by Rafael Kubelik, with Christa Ludwig, Shirley Verrett, Jon Vickers, and Louis Quilico in the principal roles, the opera was an enormous success, as was its revival in 1983, when Levine first conducted it. But when I saw it in 1983 I was so angered by what I thought were unnecessary changes to Peter Wexler's designs and Nathaniel Merrill's brilliant staging that I hardly paid attention to the music.

Eleven years later I'd calmed down about most of the staging and was now truly seized by the performances of Francoise Pollet, Maria Ewing, Gary Lakes, Dwayne Croft, and the entire company because of the absolute control that came from Levine's baton. He shaped every musical moment, making the orchestra into a single instrument of roaring force as required, and supporting, cajoling, pleading with, and giving confidence to every singer on the stage.

This was James Levine at his best, "his" orchestra, built over twenty years and now filled with fiery youngsters (only a handful left from my days) who've known no other master. This was Levine the sensitive accompanist who had learned conducting the hard way, under George Szell's severe tutelage in Cleveland, the Levine who had taken the Met out of the doldrums, and in the face of declining talents nurtured a succession of fine singers in a world generally bereft of vocal giants.

I wasn't at the performance the night of June 5, 1971, when "Big Jim," as he's sometimes called, made his Met debut conducting *Tosca* without an orchestra rehearsal, but news of this gifted youngster had already been around the music world. I knew of him because of George Szell, who told all his friends how he'd kept Levine at Cleveland for one more year than the young man thought necessary and then shoved him out the door with the comment that he'd taught him everything he needed and he was now ready to lead his own artistic life.

James Levine has always known who he was and where he intended to go. Born to a theatrical family—his great-grandfather was a cantor, his father a violinist and band-leader, his mother an actress—young James was already studying the piano at the age of four in his native Cincinnati. He made his professional debut at the keyboard six years later with the Cincinnati Symphony Orchestra. He then studied piano with Rosina Lhevinne at Juilliard and Aspen.

Despite an enormous pianistic talent, he soon found himself unalterably drawn toward the podium. "I never had a full-time piano career," he once remarked. "That seemed ridiculous to me. I practiced to be as good a pianist as possible, but I never really saw myself going around playing solo concerts on strange pianos all by myself in strange towns.

"I was a child prodigy talent. But I knew that didn't mean anything. I performed maybe two, three times a year, but there was no child prodigy career because my parents, terrific people, avoided it for me and I wanted them to."

Conducting was his goal, and when he left Cleveland and George Szell's tutelage, the young maestro began being engaged by almost every major American orchestra and a number of the first-rank European ensembles as well. He became what is known in the music world as a "repeater," being reengaged, often on the spot, almost everywhere he went.

After his 1971 Met debut, however, Rafael Kubelik and Goeran Gentele invited Levine to take on a brand-new role at the opera house—principal conductor—starting in the 1973–1974 season. By the time his appointment went into effect, Gentele's responsibilities were mine and I welcomed Levine with open arms. It was just as well, because shortly after he took up his post Kubelik resigned and Jimmy became, in fact if not in name, the company's music director.

We worked closely together all during my tenure, adding John Dexter as production director to create a troika that I think would have continued if I hadn't fallen afoul of the Met's board. The late Anthony Bliss took over from me, and under Bliss, Levine formally became music director in 1976 and in 1986, artistic director.

Levine gives himself fully to the Met, working right through the season from August to May, and continues to conduct a high proportion of the performances. He plans all the repertoire, casting, and direction. The *New York Times* finally affirmed his position by stating that, "It's Levine's Met now."

The *Times* is correct. The simple fact is that general managers come and go—Bing, Gentele, Chapin, Bliss, Crawford, Southern, and the excellent incumbent, a protégé of Bing's and mine, Joseph Volpe—but Levine rules on.

However, life at the Met is not always smooth flowing. When Levine is not conducting, the standard onstage is often deplorable. "James Levine makes sure that he gets the singers he wants for his own performances and leaves Mr. Friend [artistic administrator] to improvise the remainder of the season," charged the *Times*. Levine defends himself by saying that his critics want it both ways. "Everybody agrees about the continuous improvement of the orchestra," he notes, "but nobody has written about how you can't have that and a guest conductor's showcase at the same time." I can add a personal note: the Met could not afford to keep a top conductor for four weeks of rehearsal when such a conductor can earn a fortune nightly on the concert circuit.

On the matter of singers, though, Levine has shown himself to be an exceptional judge of talent. By some freak of nature, Italy has stopped producing Puccini voices and Germany is clean out of heldentenors. When Bayreuth needs a Wotan or Milan a Mimi, they often come to rummage Levine's American closets. He's turned out James Morris, the Wotan of the nineties, whose singularity is such that he sang the role on both Levine's Deutsche Grammophon Ring and in the concurrent EMI recording with Bernard Haitink. Kathleen Battle, another Levine discovery, was soon able to name her own fee in Mozart and Strauss parts. The present Aïda is Aprile Millo, groomed at the Met. Maria Ewing, a captivating Carmen, Salome, and Cassandra, had been spotted by Levine at a Cleveland audition where Pierre Bernac gave her the thumbs down. "Bernac didn't think I'd project [vocally]," she remembers, "but Jimmy didn't care about that. He was interested in the style and expression." Levine's singers often do not possess the enormous voices and personalities associated with opera stars. He admits that a well-cast *Butterfly,* which could be taken for granted in the 1950s, has now become "the exception rather than the rule," but in his Metropolitan Opera there are fewer black holes than at similar institutions in Europe. In an era of vocal austerity, Levine's "little leaguers" fill the gaps more than adequately. "He can make you better than you are," admitted Battle.

JAMES LEVINE

New York City
November 22, 1993

He understands the essentials of photography—the graphic elements of composition, the technical aspects behind the camera—and Levine not only becomes the subject being photographed, but also the photographer's collaborator.

—J.D.R.

On one point all the critics agree: Jimmy Levine has worked wonders with the Metropolitan Opera orchestra. In the course of the last twenty years he has steadily replaced players to the point where the orchestra is now one of the best in the United States and, alongside the Vienna Philharmonic, hands down the best opera orchestra in the world. Levine has rewarded their confidence in him by taking the orchestra to perform at Carnegie Hall and winning them the highest salaries in America.

Outside of the Met, for years Levine ran the Chicago Symphony's summertime series at Ravinia, but he now concentrates on working with the Vienna Philharmonic, which plays beautifully under his baton. In the spring of 1990 he took the Viennese on an American tour. They like him for his collegial attitude and receptive nature. "I don't get any satisfaction from telling an orchestra to do something that they don't feel for themselves," he recently told the English musicologist Norman Lebrecht. "Obviously not every member of an orchestra can agree with everything I'm asking them to do; but what is possible is to work on the music rather in the way one works on chamber music, so that the players can digest it and communicate that to the listener without the conductor having to act as a middleman. And that's very different from doing something because someone tells you to, or because you'll be fired if you don't."

He enjoys playing chamber music with both the Met orchestra and the Vienna Philharmonic, from small works to a Mozart symphonic enterprise with Vienna that's being recorded for Deutsche Grammophon. "It's very important to understand that all classical composers tried to imitate the voice . . . its natural vibrato, its tendency to express individual emotions, its tendency to tension in extreme registers"—qualities that can be especially well produced by the polished playing of the Vienna Philharmonic.

Levine began his Met career when he was twenty-eight. He's now in his early fifties. There is no telling how long this gifted and articulate man will be around to make music for his ever-widening public, but years ago he made a comment to several friends, including myself, that has stuck in my mind: "I have one real visionary dream," he said "and I feel that everything I do draws me a little closer to it. Once in a while I hear a performance which is the kind of incredible thing that must have driven composers to keep on writing music despite unbelievable personal adversities. It seems to me there is a key to this which, so far, our system has not provided. I want to try and provide it."

BIBLIOGRAPHY

I'm deeply indebted to several authors whose works added greatly to my pleasures in the task of writing this book and gave me the information I needed to round out my own portraits. I've already mentioned two—Lanfranco Rasponi's *The Last Prima Donnas* and Craig Zadan's *Sondheim and Company*. I now wish to acknowledge several others and suggest that you seek out these books for more information about the fascinating, often gnarled and frustrating, but in the end glorious world of the performing arts.

Sir Rudolf Bing. *5000 Nights at the Opera*. New York: Doubleday, 1972.

Herbert Breslin, Editor. *The Tenors*. New York: Macmillan, 1974.

James A. Drake. *Richard Tucker—A Biography*. New York: Dutton, 1984.

Norman Lebrecht. *The Maestro Myth*. New York: Birch Lane Press, Carol Publishing Group, 1991.

Helena Matheopoulos. *Maestro*. New York: Harper & Row, 1982.

Stephen E. Rubin. *The New Met in Profile*. New York: Macmillan, 1974.

Winthrop Sargeant. *Divas*. New York: Coward, McCann & Geoghegan, 1973.

Harold C. Schonberg. *The Glorious Ones*. New York: Times Books, 1985.

Beverly Sills. *Bubbles—A Self Portrait*. New York: Bobbs-Merrill, 1976.

Christopher Warwick. *The Universal Ustinov*. London: Sidgwig & Jackson, Ltd., 1990.

PHOTOGRAPHER'S ACKNOWLEDGMENTS

To Daniel and Angela Radiches—my parents,
and for Dr. Joyce Radiches—my sister.

Call it vanity, perhaps shyness—demanding schedules . . . it seemed, at times, almost impossible to procure a photo session with certain artists. For intervening on my behalf and making it possible, I am especially grateful to Carmela Bucceri Altumura, Mario Antonioli, Dennis Bergevin, Hans Boon, Syria Brown, Victor Callegari, Devereux D'Anna, Judith Goldberg, Victoria Hillebrand, Arge Keller, Bill Safka, Jane Scovell, Bob Shear, Barry Tucker, Robert Tuggle, Tina Vigano, and Martin Waldron.

With gratitude to Charlie Riecker of the Metropolitan Opera and Anna Sosenko for their encouragement; to Betty A. Prashker, editor, who saw the possibilities of such a book; to F. Amoy Allen of Crown Publishers, for her loyalty; to Paul Chung of the Lantz-Harris Agency, for his guidance; to Jeff Hildt of *Opera News,* for his cooperation.

Special thanks to designer June Bennett-Tantillo for her discerning eye; to production editor Mark McCauslin for his keen attention to detail; to production coordinator Bill Peabody for his technical expertise. Together they make one great team.

—J.D.R.